Language Server Protocol and Implementation

Supporting Language-Smart Editing and Programming Tools

T0224865

Nadeeshaan Gunasinghe
Nipuna Marcus

Apress®

Language Server Protocol and Implementation: Supporting Language-Smart Editing and Programming Tools

Nadeeshaan Gunasinghe
Walahanduwa, Sri Lanka

Nipuna Marcus
Mawathagama, Sri Lanka

ISBN-13 (pbk): 978-1-4842-7791-1
https://doi.org/10.1007/978-1-4842-7792-8

ISBN-13 (electronic): 978-1-4842-7792-8

Managing Director, Apress Media LLC: Welmoed Spahr
Acquisitions Editor: Jonathan Gennick
Development Editor: Laura Berendson
Coordinating Editor: Jill Balzano

Cover designed by eStudioCalamar

Cover image designed by Freepik (www.freepik.com)

Distributed to the book trade worldwide by Springer Science+Business Media New York, 1 New York Plaza, Suite 4600, New York, NY 10004-1562, USA. Phone 1-800-SPRINGER, fax (201) 348-4505, e-mail orders-ny@ springer-sbm.com, or visit www.springeronline.com. Apress Media, LLC is a California LLC and the sole member (owner) is Springer Science + Business Media Finance Inc (SSBM Finance Inc). SSBM Finance Inc is a **Delaware** corporation.

For information on translations, please e-mail booktranslations@springernature.com; for reprint, paperback, or audio rights, please e-mail bookpermissions@springernature.com.

Apress titles may be purchased in bulk for academic, corporate, or promotional use. eBook versions and licenses are also available for most titles. For more information, reference our Print and eBook Bulk Sales web page at http://www.apress.com/bulk-sales.

Any source code or other supplementary material referenced by the author in this book is available to readers on GitHub via the book's product page, located at www.apress.com/978-1-4842-7791-1. For more detailed information, please visit http://www.apress.com/source-code.

Printed on acid-free paper

To our beloved parents who always were behind us and Kasun Indrasiri who always was an inspiration and a role model

Table of Contents

About the Authors

Nadeeshaan Gunasinghe is Technical Lead at WSO2 and has more than five years of experience in enterprise integration, programming languages, and developer tooling. He leads the Ballerina Language Server team and is a key contributor to Ballerina, which is an open source programming language and platform for the cloud, and he is an active contributor to the WSO2 Enterprise Service Bus.

Nipuna Marcus is Technical Lead at WSO2 and has more than five years of experience in front-end development, programming languages, and developer tooling. He was a member of the Ballerina Language Server team and a key contributor to the Ballerina programming language.

About the Technical Reviewer

 **Andres Sacco** has been working as a developer since 2007 in different languages including Java, PHP, Node.js, and Android. Most of his background is in Java and the libraries or frameworks associated with this language, for example, Spring, Hibernate, JSF, and Quarkus. In most of the companies that he worked for, he researched new technologies in order to improve the performance, stability, and quality of the applications of each company.

Acknowledgments

We would first like to thank Jonathan Gennick, Assistant Editorial Director at Apress, for evaluating and accepting our proposal for this book. We would also like to thank Laura Berendson, Development Editor at Apress, and Nirmal Selvaraj, Project Coordinator, for guiding us toward the end. Andres Sacco served as the Technical Reviewer. Thank you, Andres, for making sure we did our best.

Kasun Indrasiri, Software Architect and author of *Microservices for the Enterprise* and *GRPC: Up and Running*, inspired us to work on this book and mentored us throughout the process. We are eternally grateful to Kasun Indrasiri for the guidance and support.

Finally, we would like to thank our families and parents as, without them, none of our life achievements would be possible.

Introduction

The Language Server Protocol (LSP) has been one of the most talked about topics during the past few years when it comes to the tooling for programming languages. With the advancement of the developer tools and the programming languages, developers started to rely more and more on advanced tools and enhanced language services. When we consider one of the most focused branches of developer tools which is IDEs and text editors, there are many vendors who have released various editing tools in the past couple of decades. When we consider the number of programming languages along with the number of smart editors nowadays, in order to support language intelligence among the editors, these vendors have to repeat the same thing. The Language Server Protocol was introduced to solve this particular problem, and today it has become the norm of the development tools' language intelligence provider. By adopting the LSP, tools such as text editors and integrated development environments (IDEs) could expand the capabilities and avoid the users' burden of switching between the development tools for trying new programming languages and frameworks.

This book is for the developers who are passionate about developing programming language tools. In this book, we provide the readers a comprehensive understanding about the Language Server Protocol and how to develop a Language Server from scratch. The readers will be guided with code samples to provide a better understanding about the server implementation by adhering to the user experience best practices as well as the LSP best practices. The readers are expected to use the book along with the example implementation, in order to get a better understanding about the concepts described in the book. In the example implementation, the book refers to VS Code as the client; however, the readers can use any other client and integrate the server implementation as desired.

The chapters of the book have been ordered to capture various aspects of the developer experience when it comes to the programming language tooling, and the LSP operations and features are categorized under these aspects. The readers are not overwhelmed by including the code snippets of the data structures in the LSP and it is recommended to refer to the official documentation of the Language Server Protocol for the data structures.

CHAPTER 1

Developer Tools and Language Services

Today, software development has become an area where there are higher expectations when considering the rapid development, go-to market, deployment, distribution, and similar aspects. In this book, we are going to focus on a specific technical perspective related to source code editing or, in other words, writing the software.

Early Programmable Computers

Decades before the golden age of digital computers, it all began with mechanical computers. Even though today computers can carry out various tasks, early mechanical computers could carry out a specific task. Among them, one of the most important programmable machines developed was the Jacquard loom. Jacquard loom's idea of programming the machinery was later inspired by other programmable inventions as well.

Joseph-Marie Jacquard invented the Jacquard loom[1] in 1804. The Jacquard loom was programmed by using punched cards. Different weaving patterns could be programmed by using punched cards, and the loom was automated on top of the program. Therefore, the Jacquard loom is considered the first programmable machine, and the concept of punched cards was adopted later by both Babbage as well as digital computers.

In the history of mechanical computers, the Analytical Engine developed by Charles Babbage[2] can be considered as the earliest mechanical computer. Input data was fed to the machine by means of punched cards which were used in the Jacquard

---

[1] www.columbia.edu/cu/computinghistory/jacquard.html

[2] www.computerhistory.org/babbage/

programmable loom. One of the most important aspects of the Analytical Engine is the ability to program the engine by changing the instructions on punched cards.

In both of the aforementioned examples, the medium of programming the computers was using punched cards. Not only mechanical computers but also early digital age computers used punched cards to input programs to the computer and store data. For example, if we consider computers such as IBM 360, it was the punched cards that were used to write the programs.

Code Forms and Punched Cards

For instance, let's compare how we write our programs with a programming language today with the punched card era.[3] Have you ever wondered that it might have taken hours to write a program, run it, and see the output? Have you ever tried to write a program on a piece of paper? Imagine how tedious that would be to develop even a simple "Hello world!" in such a manner? Decades before today, this is how even professional programmers used to write their programs. As briefly described in the previous section, in early days punched cards were used to store data and programs, and those cards were fed into the computer for execution. Keypunching your program to the punched card in a single run is not an easy task. Therefore, another technique called code sheets, also known as coding forms, was used. The programmers had to write their programs' instructions on the code sheets at first. Then they had to convert these instructions to a form which can be identified by the computers.

Computers could identify and process the instructions fed in the form of punched cards. A punched card operator keypunches the instructions onto the punched cards to insert them into the computer to run. If there is an error or a bug, you have to follow the same routine again and again to fix it.

Now consider a program with a number of statements and the cycle of writing, running, and fixing issues. Each time, you will get a stack of punched cards where the program is embedded into. This is the amount of work that had to be done decades ago in order to write even a simple "Hello World" program.

---

[3] www.columbia.edu/cu/computinghistory/fisk.pdf

Text Editors vs. Source Code Editors

With the advancement of technology, programmers started using various tools for writing their codes with convenience. Among these tools, text-based editors have become more popular than other options. Even though text-based tools are more popular than the others, there are other tools such as visual programming editors which allow users to write their code with graphic components. Developers can drag and drop high-level graphical constructs/basic programming constructs to build the program, and the editor auto-generates the textual code on behalf of the user. Google's Blockly is a library which allows building visual programming editors. Also, programming languages such as Prograph and visual programming environments such as Cantata[4] can be considered as tools for visual programming.

Today, when editing source codes, there are various editing tools to be chosen among. The most common choice would be a source editor, text editor, or an IDE. In one aspect, all the aforementioned choices are similar, in that all those options support text editing. But, those are completely three different tools when it comes to the editing experience. Most of the time, there is a misconception to consider that source code editors and text editors are the same even though they are not. Text editors, as the name implies, are used for editing textual content and can also be used for composing and editing source codes. Source code editors on the other hand have language sensitivity and context awareness. There are certain features incorporated into source code editors which represent language sensitivity and context awareness. Among them, auto-completion, syntax highlighting, and intelligent refactoring options such as source formatting can be shown as the most commonly used features.

Before the origin of graphical user interfaces (GUIs), command-line interface (CLI)–based text editors were popular among the developers. While CLI-based editors are command driven, GUI-based editors are menu driven. Even though GUI-based editors became popular, people continued to use CLI-based editors even today. Also, having certain expertise in using a CLI-based editor is a must when you get to work in an environment without a GUI such as a server. Today, we can install plugins and extensions for text editors, and we can convert them to behave similarly to source code editors. One such example is the Vim editor, where you can install various plugins for formatting and auto-completion for JavaScript development.[5]

---

[4] https://dl.acm.org/doi/abs/10.1145/204362.204367

[5] https://vimawesome.com/plugin/vim-javascript

3

Some examples of text-based editing tools are as follows:

- Vi

- Vim[6]

- Emacs[7]

- Notepad++[8]

- Visual Studio Code (VS Code[9])

- NetBeans[10]

- Eclipse[11]

- IntelliJ IDEA[12]

This is just a small sample of editors among numerous available options. These various editors can be categorized based on multiple factors, such as

- Language support (multi-language or specific language support)

   IDEs such as IntelliJ IDEA, Eclipse, and VS Code support multiple programming languages allowing the user to install plugins and extensions. When the Java ecosystem is considered, IntelliJ IDEA and Eclipse are the popular choices among the developers.

- Hosting environment (cloud hosted or locally hosted)

   IDEs such as Codenvy, JSFiddle, and CodePen are popular cloud-hosted IDEs. CodePen and JSFiddle have become the most widely used IDE solutions to share working code examples.

---

[6] www.vim.org/download.php

[7] www.gnu.org/software/emacs/

[8] https://notepad-plus-plus.org/

[9] https://code.visualstudio.com/

[10] https://netbeans.apache.org/

[11] www.eclipse.org/downloads/

[12] www.jetbrains.com/idea/download/

- Development type oriented (web development/mobile development/DevOps)

  Android Studio is the official IDE by Google for Android development which is built on IntelliJ IDEA. If we consider tools such as Vi and Vim, they are widely used when it comes to DevOps tasks such as server configurations.

- Extensibility and plugin support

  Users can install plugins to the VS Code editor and expand the default capabilities. For example, the VS Code marketplace has plugins for numerous programming languages.

Given the aforementioned categorization, if we consider the JVM ecosystem, the most widely used IDE is IntelliJ IDEA, while text editors such as VS Code and Vi/Vim have a lesser usage.[13] Even though we consider the JVM ecosystem here, according to the Stack Overflow Developer Survey (2021),[14] VS Code is the most commonly used text editor among the developers.

Why IDEs

Source code editing is not the only phase in the software development life cycle, which consists of a number of phases as well as associated supporting steps. In each of these steps, the stakeholders use various tools to facilitate these phases. Several such tools can be listed as follows:

- Diagramming tools (for use case identification, ER diagrams[15])

- Source code editors (Notepad++, Vim)

- Version control systems (Git,[16] SVN[17])

---

[13] https://res.cloudinary.com/snyk/image/upload/v1623860216/reports/jvm-ecosystem-report-2021.pdf

[14] https://insights.stackoverflow.com/survey/2021#integrated-development-environment

[15] https://staruml.io/

[16] https://docs.github.com/en/get-started

[17] https://subversion.apache.org/

- Debuggers (JSwat[18])

- Coverage tools (JaCoCo[19])

- Code search tools (Sourcegraph[20])

- Linters (Checkstyle[21])

- Issue trackers

- DevOps tools

- And so on

Among these tools, we can identify categories, and during the last couple of decades, various platforms and products were introduced focusing on specific categories.

When we consider the IDEs, they put numerous features together. Therefore, we can identify IDEs as an all-in-one package for a developer. This is one reason for IDEs becoming popular over time when compared to text editors. Among the incorporated features in IDEs, the following can be identified as the most widely used ones:

- Context-aware auto-completions (smart completions)

- Source refactoring options (rename references, formatting)

- Code search options (for Java, class and method search)

- Run and debug

- Code coverage

- Integrated version controlling (Git integration and SVN)

---

[18] https://github.com/nlfiedler/jswat

[19] www.eclemma.org/jacoco/

[20] https://about.sourcegraph.com/

[21] https://checkstyle.sourceforge.io/config_design.html

Language Intelligence

In the previous sections, we had a look at the various options available for source code editing. Whether it is a text editor, a source code editor, or an IDE, all of those tools have a common underlying competency to be aware of the language syntax and semantics; we call it language intelligence. Let's consider an example usage of an IDE for programming. There are numerous language-sensitive features a user uses during coding.

One of the most frequently used language intelligence features is diagnostics. For example, consider writing Java code with a missing semicolon (syntax error) and compile it. Then the compiler will stop in the middle of compilation, and the console will show the problems in the source. Listing 1-1 is an example of an erroneous Java source where there is a missing semicolon. You can copy and paste the sample code snippet in your favorite source code editor and observe how the editor represents these errors to the developer.

Listing 1-1. Invalid Java Source with a Missing Semicolon

```java
public class Greeting {
    public static void main(String[] args) {
        // Semicolon is missing in print statement
        System.out.println("Hello World")
    }
}
```

As an exercise, you can select more than one IDE/source editor and observe the diagnostic representations in those. Depending on the tool, the representation of the diagnostics can be different. Figure 1-1 is an example of the diagnostic representation for the preceding erroneous source snippet.

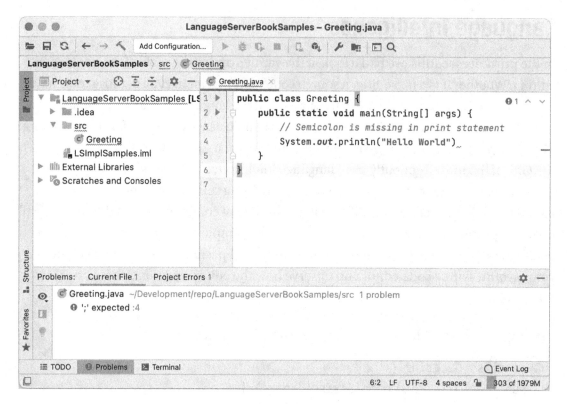

Figure 1-1. Showing diagnostics for Java in IntelliJ IDEA

When it comes to the IDEs/editors for source code editing, it is important to show the syntax or semantic errors on the fly. In order to implement the diagnostics for a particular programming language or even a configuration language such as Swagger,[22] the IDE or tooling developer needs to map the compiler's knowledge to the tooling APIs preserving the user experience.

We had a look at the diagnostics since it is one of the basic language intelligence features. Similar to the diagnostics, other features such as smart completions, refactoring (rename and formatting), code navigation, etc., play a major role in the development experience. Therefore, every developer tooling vendor pays considerable attention to language intelligence features integrated with the tools. With time, these language features were enriched with capabilities such as incorporating machine learning, artificial intelligence, and smart decompilers.[23]

---

[22] https://swagger.io/solutions/api-documentation/

[23] https://github.com/JetBrains/intellij-community/tree/master/plugins/
java-decompiler

If we consider smart suggestions in editors, tools such as Tabnine[24] allows the user to use auto-completion computed based on artificial intelligence. Tabnine computes the auto-completions for more than one language such as Java, Go, CSS, Ruby, Python, and many more. Users can install the Tabnine plugin for VS Code,[25] Intellij,[26] and even for Vim.[27] If we consider the navigation features such as go-to definitions and references, they have advanced not only to navigate within a given project or a single source but also to navigate among the archived sources such as jars and node modules. When the Java programming language is considered, external dependencies can be added as jars. From the usages of certain constructs in externally added jar bundles (classes, enums, methods, etc.), the developer might wish to navigate to the actual source and explore the implementation for more details. IDEs usually decompile the `.class` files with advanced decompilers and navigate to the referenced content.

Apart from the aforementioned examples, language intelligence has addressed various areas of the developer experience not just limiting to the textual information and navigations. With the advancement of the IDEs' and source code editors' extensibility support, the developers are provided with platform and ecosystem intelligence as well. The integration of version controlling and service deployment tools such as Git, SVN, Docker,[28] and K8s[29] are some examples of more advanced developer tools to enhance language intelligence.

Summary

From the earliest programmable computers to date, the technologies and tools used for programming computers have made a great leap. With the advancement of technologies, computer programmers started to use and develop human-readable programming languages and also more and more convenient tools to write their programs. While one

---

[24] www.tabnine.com/

[25] https://marketplace.visualstudio.com/items?itemName=TabNine.tabnine-vscode

[26] https://plugins.jetbrains.com/plugin/12798-tabnine-ai-autocomplete-javascript-c-python-ruby-rust-go-php--

[27] https://github.com/codota/tabnine-vim

[28] www.docker.com/get-started

[29] https://kubernetes.io/

of the earliest methods of composing computer programs was punched cards, today programmers use more advanced and convenient tools such as IDEs and source code editors.

In the last few decades, development tools have become more and more intelligent, convenient, and powerful. Development tool vendors started inventing and incorporating advanced technologies such as machine learning to enhance the developer experience.

The Language Server Protocol was one such powerful tool which benefited language providers as well as tooling providers to avoid repetitive, boilerplate implementation when it comes to providing language intelligence for programming languages in a given developer tool. The next chapter discusses the Language Server Protocol in detail.

CHAPTER 2

Understanding the Language Server Protocol

In Chapter 1, we discussed the evolution of computer programming and various development tools which were used to make the life of a developer easier. Among them, we are going to focus more on editors and IDEs.

Today, developers have hundreds of IDEs, text editors, and source code editors to choose from. When it comes to the editing experience and favorite tools, the users are reluctant to switch between tools. In order to avoid this, tooling vendors started to support more than one programming language, configuration language, etc.

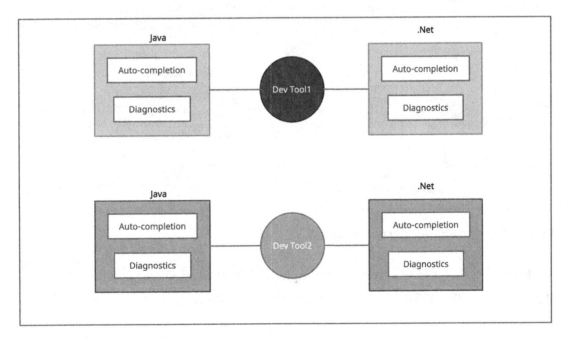

Figure 2-1. *Language provider and tooling vendor relationship*

© Nadeeshaan Gunasinghe and Nipuna Marcus 2022
N. Gunasinghe and N. Marcus, *Language Server Protocol and Implementation*,
https://doi.org/10.1007/978-1-4842-7792-8_2

Figure 2-1 shows how the relationship between language providers and tooling vendors looks. Now, if you consider a tooling vendor implementing language features such as diagnostics, auto-completions, and code navigations for a given programming language, it takes a significant effort. Different tools have different APIs to support language features, and these APIs have to consume the programming languages' APIs to consume the semantic and syntactic knowledge. This leads to using the same boilerplate implementations again and again.

In order to avoid this repetitive work, Microsoft introduced the Language Server Protocol to communicate between language clients and language smartness providers. We call the language smartness providers the Language Servers. Clients implementing the LSP can reuse the existing Language Servers to provide the language smartness without implementing it from scratch.

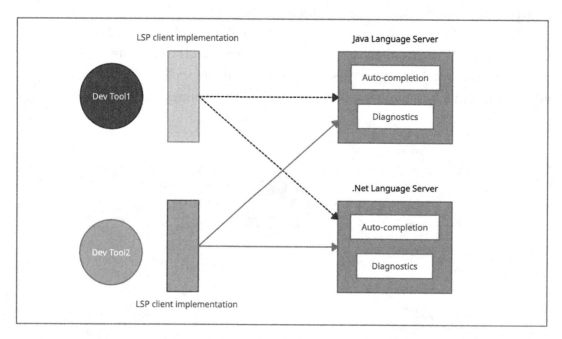

Figure 2-2. *Language Server Protocol*

Figure 2-2 shows how a given editor implementing the Language Server Protocol can support language smartness for multiple programming languages.

In the coming sections of this chapter, we will be looking at the Language Server Protocol[1] in detail.

Understanding JSON-RPC

The underlying base protocol of the Language Server Protocol is based on top of JSON-RPC 2.0. The base protocol of the Language Server contains two parts, the header part and the content part, which we will discuss in the next section.

> *JSON-RPC is a stateless, lightweight remote procedure call (RPC) protocol.*
>
> —JSON-RPC 2.0 Specification

JSON-RPC defines a set of JSON data structures and a set of rules over them. There are two main data structures defined in the specification as follows:

1. Request object

    A client sends an RPC call to a server with a request object.

2. Response object

    The server responds to the client's RPC call with a response object.

Request Object

Listing 2-1. Auto-completion Request Body Sent from the Client to the Language Server

```
{
    "jsonrpc": "2.0",
    "method": "textDocument/completion",
    "params": {
        "textDocument": {
            "uri": "file:///Users/user/hello/test.bal"
        },
```

---

[1] https://microsoft.github.io/language-server-protocol/

```
        "position": {
            "line": 59,
            "character": 0
        },
        "context": {
            "triggerKind": 1
        }
    }
    ,
    "id": 10
}
```

Listing 2-1 is an example JSON-RPC request sent from a client (editor/IDE) to a Language Server, requesting auto-completions in a given position. A request object contains the following fields.

jsonrpc

This is the JSON-RPC protocol[2] version used for the communication.

method

This is the name of the method to be invoked. The method name should be a string, and method names starting with RPC are reserved for RPC-internal methods and extensions.

params

Represents parameters for the method invocation and this field is optional. Parameters can be named parameters or positional parameters.

id

The request identifier is established by the client and used to correlate between a given request and a response. If this field is included, it MUST contain a String, a Number, or NULL.

---

[2] www.jsonrpc.org/

Notification

The request object has a variation without the `id` field which is defined as a notification, and the server MUST NOT respond to a notification.

Listing 2-2. DidOpen Notification Sent from the Client to the Language Server

```
{
    "jsonrpc": "2.0",
    "method": "textDocument/didOpen",
    "params": {
        "textDocument": {
            "uri": "file:///Users/user/hello/test.bal",
            "languageId": "ballerina",
            "version": 1,
        }
    }
}
```

Listing 2-2 is an example of a notification, which represents a notification sent from a client to a Language Server to notify a document open even in the editor.

Response Object

Listing 2-3. Hover Response Sent from the Language Server to the Client

```
{
    "jsonrpc": "2.0",
    "method": "textDocument/hover",
    "result": {
        "contents": {
            "kind": "markdown",
            "value": "Get a string result.\n  \n  \n---  \n  \n###
            Returns  \nstringReturned string value"
        }
    },
    "id": 140
}
```

The response object contains the following fields.

jsonrpc

This is the JSON-RPC protocol version used for the communication.

result

The result value is determined by the server as a response to a corresponding request method. This field MUST be included in a success scenario and MUST NOT be included in the error scenario.

error

While the result field is included in the success scenario, the error field is included in the erroneous scenario. In a response object, either the result or error fields MUST include and MUST NOT include both fields in the same response.

id

This is the identifier value of the response, and this should be the same as the id of the correlating request object.

Error Object

Listing 2-4. Method Not Found Error

```
{
    "jsonrpc": "2.0",
    "error": {
            "code": -32601,
            "message": "Method not found",
            data: {}
    },
    "id": "1"
}
```

Listing 2-4 is an example error response sent for a request with a method that is not supported by the client or the server. An error object contains the following fields.

code

This value MUST be an integer value and represents the error type that occurred. You can read more on the error codes in the JSON-RPC Specification.[3]

message

This value SHOULD be a single sentence to represent the description of the error.

data

This optional field holds additional information about the error, and the value can be either primitive or structured.

Batch

Batches allow the clients to send multiple requests to the server. Except for the notifications, the server MUST send back response objects to each of the request objects. The order of the response objects can differ from the order of the requests, and the requests and the corresponding responses should be correlated with the id.

Note   The preceding information is extracted to provide the user a glimpse of the data models and the JSON-RPC Specification. For more details, follow the official specification.[4]

---

[3] www.jsonrpc.org/specification#error_object
[4] www.jsonrpc.org/specification

Understanding the Base Protocol

The base protocol defines the header part and the content part. The header part consists of header fields, and the content part adheres to the JSON-RPC format as described in the earlier section. The following is an example message sent from a client to a Language Server:

```
Content-Length: ...\r\n
\r\n
{
     "jsonrpc": "2.0",
     "id": 1,
     "method": ...,
     "params": {

                    ...

     }
}
```

As per the example, the header part and the content part are separated by "\r\n". The header part and the content part have the following characteristics.

Header Part

- The header field and the header value are separated by ": ".
- A header field ends with a \r\n.
- The Language Server Protocol supports the Content-Length and the Content-Type header fields.

Content Part

- This follows JSON-RPC 2.0, and the jsonrpc field is set to 2.0 always.
- UTF-8 is the default encoding.

Communication Model

The Language Server Protocol's communication is protocol agnostic. We will be discussing in later chapters how to run a Language Server over standard I/O and WebSocket. There are two main communication patterns defined in the LSP as request-response and notifications. Requests and responses are correlated over the id which is initiated by either the client or the server. Notifications can be initiated by either party (client or server), and the receiving party should not respond to the notification.

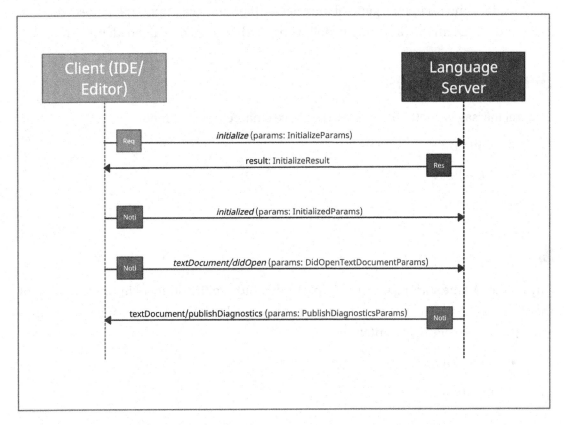

Figure 2-3. *A sample use case of how the server initialization and handshaking are happening*

The first request is sent by the client (IDE/editor) with `InitializeParams`, and the server responds with `InitializeResult`. Any request before the initialize request will be responded with an error response and notifications other than the exit notification. When the client sends the `initialize` request, the server responds to the client with the `InitializeResult`. In LSP, the initialize request can be considered as the handshake phase of the communication.

19

After the `initialize` request is sent and the server's response is received, the client sends the `initialized` notification to the server. In the depicted use case, the client then sends the `textDocument/didOpen` notification to the server to notify a file open activity in the client. Then the server publishes the diagnostics with `textDocument/publishDiagnostics` notification to the server. For any of the notifications, neither party would send a response, and a response is sent only for the requests. We will be looking at these capabilities in detail from the next chapter onward.

Each message is assigned a method name adhering to the JSON-RPC protocol specification, and except the general messages, other messages' method names are assigned a prefix. In the protocol, the following method prefixes can be identified.

General Messages

General messages' method names do not have a namespace defined:

- initialize

- initialized

- shutdown

$/

Any method name starting with the $/ prefix depends on the protocol implementation of the client or server. These methods are not guaranteed to be able to be implemented in any client or server implementation:

- cancelRequest

- progress

window

Method names starting with the `window/` prefix are used to show content on the client's user interface. For example, a showMessage notification can be used to show a message on the editor's user interface as follows. We will be discussing these methods and usages in the coming chapters in detail:

- showMessage

- showMessageRequest

- logMessage

telemetry

Telemetry events are sent from the server to the client to log the telemetry event:

- event

workspace

Method names starting with the `workspace/` prefix infer any operation which can be applied to the respective workspace. One such method is `applyEdit` which is a request sent from the server to the client for applying changes to the text documents in the workspace. Also, a `didChangeConfiguration` notification is sent from the client to the server notifying the workspace configuration changes done. We will be discussing more on this notification in the coming chapters on how we can use this notification in order to dynamically register and unregister the capabilities and more:

- applyEdit

- symbols

- configuration

textDocument

Each of the notifications and request/response pairs starting with `textDocument/` is associated with a specific text document. In order to identify the text document associated with the method, a corresponding document URI is included in the content. For example, a `textDocument/didOpen` request's parameters contain a `textDocument.uri` (as a JSON path from the content body) field. If the particular method is associated with positional information as well – such as `textDocument/definition` – the position details are also included in the content:

- didOpen

- didClose

- definition

- reference

Note The order of the requests and the responses can be different depending on the client and the server implementations. As specified in the protocol, it does not enforce an order for requests, responses, and notifications. As a general rule of thumb, the protocol specifies to consider the behaviors of the operations in the sequence, and based on that, the order can be defined/handled in the implementation.

As an example, textDocument/hover and textDocument/definition can be considered as a mutually exclusive request pair. Therefore, the server can change the order of the responses for the aforementioned requests which are received in sequence.

When textDocument/definition and textDocument/format requests are considered, it is not a good practice to change the order of the response. This is because the response for textDocument/format refactors the source code and leads to a change of position of the source code's content, which can affect the response for textDocument/definition.

Note According to the current protocol version, the lifetime of the server is controlled by the client. The client is the party to initiate the server process and kill the process.

In the coming chapters of this book, we will be looking at the Language Server Protocol in detail.

Summary

This chapter has provided a summary of the Language Server Protocol, what it is, and how it operates. You've learned about the JSON-RPC standard upon which the protocol operates, with JSON being the underlying format for requests and responses. You've seen examples of the base protocol, including headers and content. And finally, you've been introduced to the protocol-agnostic communication model. In the next chapter, you'll begin to learn how a Language Server is actually implemented.

CHAPTER 3

Implementing a Language Server

In Chapter 2, we discussed the Language Server Protocol and how it works. In this chapter, let's look at how to implement a Language Server and what tools we need to implement it. When implementing a Language Server, it is not only the language features we need to focus on, but also we should have an underlying protocol implementation. As we discussed in Chapter 2, the Language Server Protocol is implemented on top of the JSON-RPC protocol specification. Therefore, the server implementation has to be done along with the JSON-RPC protocol implementation. We will have a look into these in the coming sections of this chapter.

In this book, we are going to refer to the Ballerina[1] programming language which is the reference language we are going to provide the language smartness. For the reference language, we choose Ballerina for a few reasons:

1. It is easy to understand, and all the common language features discussed in the Language Server Protocol can be implemented for Ballerina.

2. Using a new language as the reference will allow the users to get convinced about the gravity of the protocol.

3. Rich compiler APIs of Ballerina make the implementation easy.

Also, our Language Server implementation will be done with `Java`, and the client implementation will be done with `Typescript`. In this book, we assume that the reader has an intermediate knowledge about programming and familiarity with any programming language. Also, we chose a different set of programming languages for

---

[1] https://ballerina.io/

© Nadeeshaan Gunasinghe and Nipuna Marcus 2022
N. Gunasinghe and N. Marcus, *Language Server Protocol and Implementation*,
https://doi.org/10.1007/978-1-4842-7792-8_3

the client implementation, server implementation, and as the reference programming language, in order to emphasize the true power of the Language Server Protocol. This means we can implement the Language Server Protocol using different technologies for any programming language as long as we adhere to the protocol specification.

Throughout this book, we are going to discuss and implement the Language Server Protocol version `3.16.0` which is the latest protocol version at the time of writing this book. However, all the concepts we are discussing here can be applied to any protocol version. Also, it is important to mention that we are not going to cover the Moniker feature of the Language Server Protocol since it is a part of the Language Server Indexing Format (LSIF[2]).

Tools and Dependencies

First of all, in order to develop a Language Server for a language, you need an implementation of the Language Server Protocol. There are two ways. You can either implement the Language Server Protocol yourself or use an existing implementation. Here, what we are going to do is to use an existing protocol implementation. When deciding whether to implement the underlying protocol from scratch or use an existing implementation, it is important to keep in mind the complexity of the implementation, the time and effort it will take to implement the full specification. It is also a major requirement to maintain the backward compatibility of protocol versions. And most importantly, it is always encouraged to reuse without reinventing the wheel if there are already implemented and maintained implementations. When choosing an underlying protocol implementation, it is important to keep the following in mind:

1. Compliance with the JSON-RPC 2.0 protocol specification

2. Supported Language Server Protocol versions

3. Supported set of features in the Language Server Protocol

4. Extendability support

5. Error handling

---

[2]https://microsoft.github.io/language-server-protocol/specifications/lsif/0.4.0/ specification/

After considering the aforementioned facts, we are going to use the LSP4J[3] library which is a Java implementation for the Language Server Protocol. The LSP4J project is developed and maintained by the Eclipse organization. The project is published under two public licenses:

1. Eclipse Public License v. 2.0[4]

2. Eclipse Distribution License v. 1.0[5]

When we consider the LSP4J implementation, it is not only a Language Server Protocol implementation, but also it can be used as a generic JSON-RPC implementation for Java. This allows us to extend the Language Server Protocol's capabilities and introduce custom services and operations to the base protocol. We will be discussing this aspect in Chapter 11. Also, this library includes the Debug Adapter Protocol (DAP[6]) implementation, which will be very useful for a tool developer of a programming language to have all necessary components in one library.

Next, we have to find a suitable IDE for developing your Language Server. We're gonna use Java 11 to develop the Language Server as it is the latest Java version at the time; hence, let's get an IDE that supports this version of Java. Also, later we are going to develop a sample VS Code extension to support the Language Server that we are writing; hence, we need to install VS Code, Node.js, and TypeScript as well.

Building the Project

Before you start to set up, you need to clone the project's repository locally. The project repository is hosted in GitHub and can be accessed via https://github.com/lsp-and-implementation/language-server; this book will be referring to the tag release_1.0.0, and the latest improvements will be available in the master branch. First of all, let's clone the repo to your local environment. Execute the git clone <repository_url> to clone the repository. Also, before you clone the repository, make sure that you have installed git as well. You can follow Git's official documentation to download[7] git and install.

---

[3] https://github.com/eclipse/lsp4j
[4] www.eclipse.org/org/documents/edl-v10.php
[5] www.eclipse.org/legal/epl-2.0/
[6] https://microsoft.github.io/debug-adapter-protocol/
[7] https://git-scm.com/book/en/v2/Getting-Started-Installing-Git

We use Gradle as the build tool for our project. You can either use a package manager to install Gradle or manually install it. The official Gradle documentation[8] guides you through the installation step by step.

The project contains three main components, server implementation, launchers, and client implementation, as shown in Listing 3-1.

Listing 3-1. Repository Structure

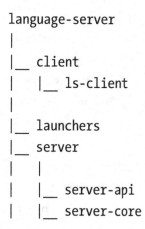

```
language-server
|
|__ client
|   |__ ls-client
|
|__ launchers
|__ server
|   |
|   |__ server-api
|   |__ server-core
```

In order to build the server component, execute the `./gradlew clean build` from the repository root. Once you execute the command, the server-api, server-core, and launchers will be built, and it will create an uber jar. Then the generated uber jar will be copied to the `client/ls-client` directory. Once you build the client, this uber jar will be copied to the VS Code extension artifact (.vsix).

In order to develop the client implementation, we recommend using the VS Code editor. Now let's have a look at how to build the client. Our client implementation is done as a VS Code extension, and in order to build the extension, you need to have npm and node installed. The node version should be `12.0` at least and npm `6.14` at least. You can use the node version manager (nvm[9]) to easily install both node and npm. Once you install node and npm, execute the `npm run build` command to build the plugin. This will generate the VS Code extension artifact. You can install the *vsix* artifact to experience how the Language Server works.

---

[8] https://gradle.org/install/
[9] https://heynode.com/tutorial/install-nodejs-locally-nvm

Compatibility with Ballerina

The initial version of the Language Server implementation is done for the Ballerina SwanLake-Beta-3 version. In order to run the Language Server with Ballerina, download Ballerina SwanLake-Beta3 from the official website[10] and install. If you need to test with the latest versions of the Ballerina release, you can follow the instructions in the Language Server repository's README.md.

After installing Ballerina, go to the user settings[11] of VS Code and set the ballerina. home user setting to the location of the installed Ballerina version. If you install Ballerina from the standard distribution, you can find the Ballerina home directory by executing the bal home command.

Debugging the Client and the Server

When you are changing the client implementation and server implementation, you might need to debug both client and server runtimes. In order to do so, you have to follow a few simple steps. Under the client/ls-client/.vscode directory, you can find a file called launch.json. There you can find a configuration option named LSDEBUG. Change the value to true and now run the client in debug mode. This will launch a VS Code instance in which the Language Server will be running in remote debug mode.

Now go to your favorite IDE which you use for Java development and create a remote debug configuration on port 5005. Now you can debug the running client and the server implementation.

Understanding the Main Components

As discussed in the previous section, there are three main components in the implementation. Now let's have a brief look at each of the components.

---

[10] https://ballerina.io/downloads/swan-lake-archived/

[11] https://code.visualstudio.com/docs/getstarted/settings

Server API

The implementation contains a module called `server-api`. The server API module contains all the APIs which we are using in our core implementation. We are keeping all the interfaces of the main components inside this module for maintainability, and also this allows us the flexibility to extend individual language features with ease. One of the most important designs we are following in our implementation is, for each of the language feature implementations, we are using a context instance to carry information between method calls. For example, let's consider the `textDocument/completion` operation where we have the `BalCompletionContext` interface which extends from the `BalPosBasedContext` interface. Listing 3-2 shows the structure of both contexts.

Listing 3-2. Example Context Interfaces

```
public interface BalPosBasedContext extends BalTextDocumentContext {
    List<Symbol> visibleSymbols();

    /**
     * Set the token at the completion's cursor position.
     *
     * @param token {@link Token} at the cursor
     */
    void setTokenAtCursor(Token token);
    /**
     * Get the token at the cursor.
     *
     * @return {@link Token}
     */
    Token getTokenAtCursor();

    /**
     * Set the node at cursor.
     *
     * @param node {@link NonTerminalNode} at the cursor position
     */
    void setNodeAtCursor(NonTerminalNode node);
```

```
    /**
     * Get the node at the completion request triggered cursor position.
     *
     * @return {@link NonTerminalNode} at the cursor position
     */
    NonTerminalNode getNodeAtCursor();

    /**
     * Set the cursor position as an offset value according to the syntax tree.
     *
     * @param offset of the cursor
     */
    void setCursorPositionInTree(int offset);

    /**
     * Get the cursor position as an offset value according to the syntax tree.
     *
     * @return {@link Integer} offset of the cursor
     */
    int getCursorPositionInTree();

    /**
     * Get the cursor position where the auto completion request triggered.
     *
     * @return {@link Position} cursor position
     */
    Position getCursorPosition();
}

// Completion context interface
public interface BalCompletionContext extends BalPosBasedContext {
    CompletionCapabilities clientCapabilities();
}
```

When the server receives the request, we calculate certain data from the completion parameters, such as the visible symbols and the syntax node at the cursor position. Once we calculate this information, we encapsulate all these in a context instance and pass it among the method calls. This allows us to keep our internal APIs clean and cache the computed information for a request and reuse them until the end of the request's life cycle.

Also, we have an interface for the `DiagnosticsPublisher`, which will be used to publish diagnostics to the client. We added a separate implementation since the server can publish the diagnostics at any place, and this publisher instance should be aware of the previously published diagnostics to clear them when we publish a new set of diagnostics. This also means that a given Language Server instance will have a single diagnostic publisher.

The `ClientLogManager` interface provides a set of generic APIs to the server to publish various types of logs. When we publish diagnostics via protocol operations, we need to generate a specific set of data models which is common. Therefore, a single logger instance is going to be used within the server's core implementation. Listing 3-3 shows the structure of the log manager interface.

Listing 3-3. ClientLogManager Interface

```
public interface ClientLogManager {
    /**
     * Log an Info message to the client.
     *
     * @param message {@link String}
     */
    void publishInfo(String message);

    /**
     * Log a Log message to the client.
     *
     * @param message {@link String}
     */
    void publishLog(String message);

    /**
     * Log an Error message to the client.
     *
```

```
 * @param message {@link String}
 */
void publishError(String message);

/**
 * Log a Warning message to the client.
 *
 * @param message {@link String}
 */
void publishWarning(String message);

void showErrorMessage(String message);
}
```

One of the most important APIs in the implementation is the `CompilerManager`. When it comes to the Ballerina language, we can create an in-memory project model for a given Ballerina project. When we consider Language Server implementation perspectives and client behaviors, we have to cache in-memory project models within the Language Server's core implementation. Imagine that the client does not automatically save the source changes to the disk. In such cases, how are we going to access the latest version of the project to generate the required semantic information? Also, even though the client periodically saves the source content to the disk, what would be the cost of reading the source from the file system for each Language Server operation such as auto-completions? The CompilerManager will be caching the projects in memory and allow the server to access the latest source changes faster. Also, we can provide a set of utility APIs such as syntax tree access, semantic model access, etc., when given a document URI.

Server Core

The server core includes the core implementation of the Language Server. This implementation includes the implementations of all the interfaces we discussed in the previous section. Other than that, the Language Server instance implementation, `BalLanguageServer`, also resides within the core component. The `BalLanguageServer` implementation extends the `LanguageServer` interface of `lsp4j`. In Chapter 11, we will see a variation of this implementation, allowing us to extend the base protocol. We are going to discuss in later chapters the general messages of the Language Server Protocol such as `initialize`, `initialized`, `shutdown`, etc. All these initial handshake-related message APIs are residing within the BalLanguageServer implementation. You will get the chance to refer to the implementation in detail in the coming chapters.

Next, we have two main implementations within the core component which are the namespace services. In the previous chapter, we discussed various namespaces for Language Server operations, such as `textDocument` and `workspace`. For each of these namespaces, there is an implementation as `BalTextDocumentService` and `BalWorkspaceService` respectively extending `TextDocumentService` and `WorkspaceService` interfaces in lsp4j. For each of the operations within the Language Server Protocol, there is an associated method in these interfaces. Each of the methods' input parameters defines the corresponding Language Server operation's input parameters, and the return type defines the response. These operations can either be a request or a response. In Listing 3-4, you can see there are two getters defined in the BalLanguageServer class to return the instances of the text document service and the workspace service. We will also be having a look at how to register such new services to extend the Language Server Protocol in Chapter 11.

Listing 3-4. Getters for the Service Instances

```
public class BalLanguageServer implements BalExtendedLanguageServer,
LanguageClientAware {
    ...
    @Override
    public TextDocumentService getTextDocumentService() {
        return this.textDocumentService;
    }

    @Override
    public WorkspaceService getWorkspaceService() {
        return this.workspaceService;
    }
    ...
}
```

Client Implementation

The next important component we need to have a look at is the client implementation. The client implementation follows the VS Code extension development template as described in the official documentation. In this guide, we are not going to analyze the client implementation since we expect the reader to integrate the developed Language Server with any desired client implementation. If you would like to have a more detailed explanation, you can follow the official VS Code extension development guide[12] along with the client implementation.

Summary

In this chapter, we had a brief look at the project repository and the main components of the implementation. Also, we had a look at the build tools and required development tools to build and develop the Language Server example we are going to refer to throughout this book.

The user can go through the source code and do alterations and improvements to the existing implementation to create their own Language Server implementation. Although the compiler internals are focused on the Ballerina language, the server can easily migrate to another language semantics.

Also, in this chapter, we had a look at each of the main implementation classes. The BalLanguageServer implementation and service implementation details will give you the initial understanding required to get started with the implementation which we are going to discuss from the next chapter onward. For a better understanding of lsp4j APIs and usages, you can refer to the lsp4j[13] guidelines.

We have looked at the basics of the Language Server Protocol and how to get started with the implementation. Now we are ready to have an in-depth understanding about Language Server features and associated concepts. In the next chapter, we are going to dive in to understand general messages and window operations of the Language Server Protocol.

---

[12] https://code.visualstudio.com/api/get-started/your-first-extension
[13] https://github.com/eclipse/lsp4j

CHAPTER 4

General Messages

In this chapter, we are going to have a look at general messages and window operations in the Language Server Protocol. We will be looking at how the Language Server implementation is going to utilize these capabilities at the protocol handshake and also use window operations to improve the developer experience.

General Messages

Initialize

An initialize request is the first request sent from the client to the server, and the client-server handshake is initiated with this request. Any of the requests sent before the initialize request is responded with an error response, and any of the notifications which are sent before the initialize request will be dropped. The only exception is for the exit notification sent by the client to the server. As per the protocol, the server will send the error with code: -32002. Table 4-1 explains the error codes defined by the protocol.

Table 4-1. *Error Codes*

Error Code	Description
-32700	ParseError – The JSON-RPC message parsing failed
-32600	InvalidRequest – The JSON-RPC request is invalid and does not conform to the JSON-RPC scheme
-32601	MethodNotFound – Could not find a method specified with the message
-32602	InvalidParams – Provided parameters are invalid
-32603	InternalError – Any other internal error

(continued)

© Nadeeshaan Gunasinghe and Nipuna Marcus 2022
N. Gunasinghe and N. Marcus, *Language Server Protocol and Implementation*,
https://doi.org/10.1007/978-1-4842-7792-8_4

Table 4-1. *(continued)*

Error Code	Description
-32099	`jsonrpcReservedErrorRangeStart` – This is the starting range of the error codes which are reserved for the JSON-RPC base protocol
-32002	`ServerNotInitialized` – An error is thrown when the server receives a request or notification before the server is initiated (before receiving the initialize request)
-32001	`UnknownErrorCode` – An error can be thrown when the server receives a request or notification before the server is initiated
-32000	`jsonrpcReservedErrorRangeEnd` – This is the end of the range of the error codes which are reserved for the JSON-RPC base protocol
-32899	`lspReservedErrorRangeStart` – This is the starting range of the error codes which are reserved for the Language Server Protocol
-32801	`ContentModified` – The server detects an internal state change while calculating the result for a request which invalidates the request such as the project's state change
-32800	`RequestCancelled` – A request has been cancelled, and the sending party will not accept the response
-32800	lspReservedErrorRangeEnd – This is the end of the range of the error codes which are reserved for the Language Server Protocol

Before responding to the `initialize` request, the server cannot send any notifications to the client. Only the following are allowed during the `initialize` request

- window/showMessage

  This is a notification that is sent from the server to the client, and upon receiving the notification, the client shows a message on the user interface.

- window/logMessage

  This is a notification sent by the server to the client in order to show a log message on the output channel.

- telemetry/event

Telemetry events emitted by the server for various meta-information captured such as usage statistics.

We will be looking at an example of sending notifications, and we will be discussing these notifications later in this chapter under the "Window Operations" section.

Let's have a look at an example use case on how to handle the initialize request in the Language Server implementation.

The following is a trace log extracted for the initialize request in our Language Server example. Now let's have a look at the InitializeParams in Listing 4-1.

Listing 4-1. Trace Message for InitializeParams

```
Params: {
            "processId": 2179,
            "rootPath": "/Users/langserver/projectLS",
            "rootUri": "file:///Users/langserver/projectLS",
            "capabilities": {...},
            "trace": "verbose",
            "initializationOptions": {
                "enableDocumentationCodeLenses": false
            },
            "workspaceFolders": [
                {
                    "uri":"file:///Users/langserver/projectLS",
                    "name": "projectLS"
                }
            ]
        ...
}
```

The client sends InitializeParams as the request parameters which contains the following properties.

The processId property specifies the parent process ID which started the Language Server process. If the server is not started by another process, the value would be null and otherwise an integer.

The clientInfo property specifies the information of the client. This information is necessary for the servers when they need additional meta-information about the clients as well as for logging rich messages for the user. The clientInfo property contains two child properties as `clientInfo.name` and `clientInfo.version`, which specify the client name and the client's version, respectively.

The `locale` property specifies the current locale which is being used by the client. The servers can make use of this value to show the developers a locale-based information for the users. For example, based on the locale the servers can change the language of the messages logged into the console.

The `workspaceFolders` contains a list of `WorkspaceFolder` data structures for each of the folders opened in the workspace of the client. In our example, there is one open folder in the workspace. It is important to know that the concept of the workspace will depend on the client implementation. The `rootUri` property has been deprecated in favor of the `workspaceFolders` property, and it is recommended to depend on the `workspaceFolders`.

The `initializationOptions` allow the client to send additional options at the server initialization. For example, we are going to set a custom option to enable and disable documentation-related code lenses in the server. Listing 4-2 shows how to set initialization options at the client side (in our scenario, VS Code). The captured trace log in Listing 4-1 shows how these `initializationOptions` are sent to the server. From a plugin/extension to another, developers can add various customized options such as formatting options, customized options for code actions, caching limits, etc. One option to communicate these configuration options via the client to the server is using the `initializationOptions` during the Language Server connection initialization. Other than that, we can use the `workspace/configurations` request sent from the server to the client and `workspace/didChangeConfiguration` notification sent from the client upon configuration changes.

Listing 4-2. Add initializationOptions in VS Code Extensions (extension.ts)

```
let clientOptions: LanguageClientOptions = {
    // Register the server for ballerina documents
    documentSelector: [
        { scheme: 'file', language: 'ballerina' }
    ],
    // Set the initialization options
    initializationOptions: {
```

```
            enableDocumentationCodeLenses: false
    }
};
```

This `clientCapabilities` property specifies the list of capabilities facilitated by the client – the editor or the tool. Let's have a look at the types of capabilities exposed during the initialization.

The `clientCapabilities.textDocument` property specifies the client capabilities associated with the text document and represented by the `TextDocumentClientCapabilities` data model.

The `clientCapabilities.workspace` property specifies the workspace capabilities provided by the client.

The client capabilities which are specific to the window are listed under the `window` property. These capabilities are as follows:

- workDoneProgress

- showMessage

- showDocument

Window operations are one of the most helpful features which can be used to provide a rich developer experience. The server can show messages, open files upon code actions/command executions, as well as show the progress of background tasks such as loading indexes. We will be looking at these operations later in this chapter under the "Window Operations" section.

The `general` property specifies the general client capabilities supported by the client. The `general.regularExpressions` property specifies the client capabilities associated with the regular expression engine used by the client. The `general.markdown` property specifies the client capabilities associated with the markdown parser used by the client. These properties are important for the server in scenarios such as when generating markdown documentation for the hover response. Since markdown parser specifications can have feature deviations, depending on this property, the server can specify how to generate a rich markdown content.

The `experimental` property specifies experimental/preview features under development.

In this section, we will not be going through each and every data model associated with the capabilities, but we will be looking into these data models along with their respective features in the coming chapters of this book. In later chapters, for each of the capabilities/features which we are going to discuss, we will be specifying the client capabilities associated with the particular capability. When referring to client capabilities, the user can refer to the BalLanguageServer class and the initialize method to access the client capabilities.

These configurations allow Language Server implementation to conditionally change execution paths. One of the most common use cases is dynamic capability registration. Listing 4-3 shows how we can dynamically register the onTypeFormatting. It is common for the servers to dynamically register capabilities upon the initialized notification.

Listing 4-3. Dynamically Register onTypeFormatting (DynamicCapabilitySetter.java)

```
public void registerOnTypeFormatting() {
    Optional<ClientCapabilities> clientCapabilities = this.lsContext.
    clientCapabilities();

    if (clientCapabilities.isEmpty()) {
        // Client capabilities are not saved
        return;
    }

    OnTypeFormattingCapabilities onTypeFormatting =
            clientCapabilities.get()
            .getTextDocument().getOnTypeFormatting();
    if (!onTypeFormatting.getDynamicRegistration()) {
        /*
        client does not support dynamic registration for
        ontype formatting. Gracefully fall back
        */
        return;
    }
    // Generate the registration options
    DocumentOnTypeFormattingRegistrationOptions opts =
    new DocumentOnTypeFormattingRegistrationOptions();
    opts.setFirstTriggerCharacter("}");
    opts.setMoreTriggerCharacter(Collections.singletonList(";"));
```

```
String method = Method.ON_TYPE_FORMATTING.getName();
/*
We use method name for both id and the method and we use the same for
unregister a capability
*/
Registration reg = new Registration(method, method);
List<Registration> regList = Collections.singletonList(reg);
RegistrationParams regParams =
      new RegistrationParams(regList);

// Send the register request and ignore the void result
serverContext.getClient().registerCapability(regParams);
}
```

It is not necessary for the clients to support dynamic capability registration. In cases where dynamic registration is not supported by the client, the recommended option is to register the capabilities statically via the InitializeResult as shown in Listing 4-4.

The workspace capabilities specify the operations supported by the client which apply to the workspace. Some of these capabilities are as follows:

- applyEdit support

  This is a server-initiated request sent to the client to perform workspace edit operations such as changing document content.

- symbol support

  A workspace symbol request is sent by the client to the server for requesting symbols in the workspace.

- executeCommand support

  This is a client-initiated request which is sent to the server for carrying out various operations associated with the command. Code actions can be considered as one of the most frequently used use cases.

We are going to look at these operations in detail later in this book.

Generating the InitializeResult

When the server receives the `initialize` request, the server replies with the
`InitializeResult`. Listing 4-4 shows setting the result with server capabilities, and
Listing 4-5 shows a trace log extracted for the response to an initialize request.

Listing 4-4. Register Capabilities at Server Initialization (BalLanguageServer.java)

```java
public class BalLanguageServer implements LanguageServer {
    @Override
    public CompletableFuture<InitializeResult>
                    initialize(InitializeParams params) {
        return CompletableFuture.supplyAsync(() -> {
                serverContext.setClientCapabilities(params.
                getCapabilities());
                ServerCapabilities sCapabilities = new
                ServerCapabilities();

                TextDocumentSyncOptions documentSyncOption =
                    ServerInitUtils.getDocumentSyncOption();
                CompletionOptions completionOptions =
                    ServerInitUtils.getCompletionOptions();
                sCapabilities.setTextDocumentSync(documentSyncOption);
                sCapabilities.setCompletionProvider(completionOptions);

                return new InitializeResult(sCapabilities);
            });
        }
}
```

Listing 4-5. InitializeResult Trace Log

```json
{
    "capabilities": {
        "textDocumentSync": 1,
        "completionProvider": {
            "triggerCharacters": [
                ":",
```

```
                    ".",
                    ">",
                    "@"
                ]
        },
    }
    serverInfo: {
      // goes here
    }
}
```

Initialized

The `initialized` notification is sent from the client to the server after receiving the response for the `initialize` request. The client is not supposed to send any request or notification before sending the initialized notification.

During the implementation, the server can utilize the receiving of this notification to carry out various server startup tasks. For example, dynamically registering capabilities, initializing internal caches, and initializing indexes can be seen as the most common use cases. Depending on the implementation, the tasks to be carried out can be different.

Listing 4-6. Handling the initialized notification (BalLanguageServer.java)

```
@Override
public void initialized(InitializedParams params) {
        // Registering the onTypeFormatting capability
        this.dynamicCapabilitySetter.registerOnTypeFormatting(this.
        serverContext);
        // Other initializing tasks can be handled here
}
```

Shutdown

The `shutdown` request is sent from the client to the server to inform of a shutdown. Upon receiving the request, the server should not immediately exit the current server process and should exit upon the exit notification sent from the client.

During the server's lifetime, there can be resources being locked sometimes such as file system resources, and those resources need to be gracefully released before the server exits. Similar use cases such as saving a snapshot of the current index and dumping caches can be carried out during this phase. The Language Server can gracefully initiate the exit process when it receives the shutdown request and exit the running process later when it receives the exit notification.

Exit

The client sends the exit notification to the server, and the server is supposed to exit the running process once this notification is received. As the previous section described, the server can finish the cleanup tasks during the shutdown request and then exit the process gracefully at the exit notification. Listing 4-7 shows the exit process in the example server implementation. In our scenario, we execute the System.exit() to kill the running Java process. Depending on the implementation, sometimes the Language Server process will not be started by the client, for example, when we have a WebSocket-based Language Server implementation. In such cases, the WebSocket server can initiate a separate Language Server instance for each of the clients, and in such cases, exiting the entire process will not be ideal.

Listing 4-7. Graceful Exit of the Server Process (BalLanguageServer.java)

```
@Override
public CompletableFuture<Object> shutdown() {
        this.shutdownInitiated = true;
        return CompletableFuture.supplyAsync();
}

@Override
public void exit() {
        // the flag is true when the client sends the shutdown request
        // Gracefully exit server process
        if (this.shutdownInitiated) {
              System.exit(0);
        } System.exit(1);
}
```

Window Operations

ShowMessage

The `window/showMessage` notification is sent from the server to the client, and upon receiving the notification, the client shows a message on the user interface. Depending on the client's user experience, the message showing can be different from one client to another. When using window operations such as `showMessage`, `showMessageRequest`, and `logMessage` during the server implementation, the developer has to be careful on when to use the show message and log message operations without disturbing the user experience. Figure 4-1 shows how info messages are shown on VS Code. Listing 4-8 shows how to send the `showMessage` notification to the client on a successful server initiation when the client sends the `initialized` notification.

Figure 4-1. *showMessage notification shown on the VS Code user interface*

The server sends the `MessageParams` data structure to the client containing the message to be shown, and the server can set the `message` property. Also, the server can set the type of message by setting the `messageType` property. The message types are as follows:

- Info
- Log
- Error
- Warning

Listing 4-8. Send the showMessage Notification to the Client
(BalLanguageServer.java)

```
@Override
public void initialized(InitializedParams params) {
        // Registering the onTypeFormatting capability
        this.dynamicCapabilitySetter.registerOnTypeFormatting();
        // Other initializing tasks can be handled here
        MessageParams messageParams = new MessageParams();
          messageParams.setMessage("Server Initiated!");
          messageParams.setType(MessageType.Info);
          this.client.showMessage(messageParams);
}
```

ShowMessageRequest

The server sends the window/showMessageRequest to the client to display a message on
the user interface as the showMessage notification and also allows the server to wait for
an action from the client. This is an important feature for the servers to get user consent
before executing actions. For example, the server can ask the user's consent to open a
file within a project. In our example use case, if a Ballerina project is failing to load due
to an error in the Ballerina.toml file, we are going to ask the user's consent to open the
Ballerina.toml file.

The client capabilities of the showMessageRequest specify whether the client can
support additional properties (messageActionItem.additionalPropertiesSupport)
and send to the server with the response.

Generating the Request

The server creates a ShowMessageRequestParams data structure as the request
parameters for the client.

The message and messageType properties are the same as we discussed in
the showMessage notification. The optional actions property specifies an array of
MessageActionItems. A MessageActionItem is a data structure which contains a title that
is shown as the available set of inputs from the user.

As a response, the client sends a MessageActionItem if the user selects an available
option and null if otherwise.

The example in Listing 4-9 sends the showMessageRequest to the client asking whether to open the Ballerina.toml file when there is an error in loading the project.

Listing 4-9. Send the showMessageRequest to the Client (BallerinaCompilerManager.java)

```
private Optional<Project> buildProject(Path path) {
    try {
            ...
        // Build the project

        if (this.projectContainsTomlDiagnostics(project)) {
            ShowMessageRequestParams params = new
            ShowMessageRequestParams();
            MessageActionItem openBalToml = new
            MessageActionItem("Open Ballerina.toml");
            params.setMessage("Ballerina.toml contains Errors");
            params.setActions(Collections.
            singletonList(openBalToml));
            this.client.showMessageRequest(params)
            .whenComplete((messageActionItem, throwable) -> {
                    ShowDocumentParams documentParams = new
                    ShowDocumentParams();
                    documentParams.setExternal(false);
                    documentParams.setUri(project.sourceRoot().
                    resolve("Ballerina.toml").toUri().toString());
                    documentParams.setTakeFocus(true);
                    client.showDocument(documentParams);
            });
        }
            this.projectsMap.putIfAbsent(packageRoot, project);

            return Optional.ofNullable(project);
        } catch (ProjectException e) {
            return Optional.empty();
        }
    }
}
```

ShowDocument

The server can send the showDocument request to the client asking to show a document on the editor. One important capability of this feature is that the Language Server Protocol allows to open external documents such as URIs as well.

Client capabilities (ShowDocumentClientCapabilities) specify whether the client supports the showDocument operation by setting the support property to true.

Generating the Request

The server generates a ShowDocumentParams data structure as the request parameters.

The uri property specifies the document URI to be opened. This can either be a text document or an external document source such as a web resource.

The external property specifies whether the particular document to be opened is an external web resource or a text document. Depending on this property, the client can decide the form of opening the particular resource. In the case of an external resource, the client will open the resource in the default web browser.

The takeFocus property specifies whether the client needs to open the resource and then change the focus to the particular resource. When using this feature, there are certain scenarios where the server does not need to interrupt the developer experience. Consider a use case where the server generates debug logs after a code action execution. The server can ask the client to show a message to get the consent to open the document. In such scenarios, the server can either open the log file in a separate tab while the user's focus is on the current tab or open the log and change the focus to the particular tab. Depending on the use case, the server should identify whether to change the focus or otherwise.

The selection property specifies the range of the document to be selected in case the document is not a web resource. Refer Listing 4-9 for the implementation.

LogMessage

The server sends the window/logMessage notification to the client to show a log message on the output channel. In VS Code, we can create a separate output channel for the plugin, and for a cleaner logging approach, it is a convenient option to have a separate channel. When the server sends the logMessage notification, the client will show the particular log message on the output channel.

The LogMessageParams are sent to the client where the message property specifies the message to be displayed, and the messageType specifies the kind of message, such as Info or Warning, which is the same as we discussed in the "showMessage" section.

Listing 4-10 specifies how to use the logMessage notification to show a successful server initiation at the startup of the Language Server.

Listing 4-10. Send the logMessage Notification to the Client (BalLanguageServer.java)

```
@Override
public void initialized(InitializedParams params) {
        // Registering the onTypeFormatting capability
        this.dynamicCapabilitySetter.registerOnTypeFormatting();
        // Other initializing tasks can be handled here
        MessageParams messageParams = new MessageParams();
        messageParams.setMessage("Server Initiated!");
        messageParams.setType(MessageType.Info);
        // log the message on output channel
        this.client.logMessage(messageParams);
}
```

Progress/Create

The server sends the window/workDoneProgress/create request to the client for creating a work done progress. The WorkDoneProgressCreateParams contains the token to identify the particular progress request.

Progress/Cancel

The server sends the window/workDoneProgress/cancel request to the client for cancelling a work done progress. The WorkDoneProgressCancelParams contains the token to identify the particular progress request.

We will be looking more into progress done requests and use cases in later chapters of this book.

Summary

In this chapter, we had a look at general messages where we can utilize them at the server initialization as well as gracefully shutting down the server. It is an important aspect to register the server capabilities at the Language Server's startup. The servers get the freedom to either register the capabilities at the initialize request or dynamically register them at the initialized notification. This capability registration approach can depend on the housekeeping tasks to be carried out, metadata processing, indexing, and similar tasks to be carried out in the server.

Window operations can be used to provide a better developer experience while communicating various status messages with the developer. When using window operations, it is important to keep in mind not to overuse the features and interrupt the developer experience. In later chapters, we will be looking at scenarios where we can combine the window operations with other Language Server features such as code actions.

After having an in-depth understanding about general messages and the window operations, now we are ready to dive into language features supported by the Language Server Protocol. In the next chapter, we are going to look at text synchronization features and capabilities provided by the Language Server.

CHAPTER 5

Text Synchronization

In this chapter, we are going to have a look at text synchronization capabilities available in the Language Server Protocol. When the user opens a document in the client (editor/ IDE), source editing is initiated through the client. Clients are responsible for syncing the source content with the file system or maintaining an in-memory copy. Not all clients automatically sync the source content periodically with the file system. Clients such as Vim keep the up-to-date content in memory, and the user can decide whether to persist the content or discard them (users can install plugins such as vim-auto-save[1] or configure the Vim editor to periodically save buffer on text changes to sync the content). Clients such as VS Code and Eclipse expose configuration options for the user to determine whether to auto-save the content or not.

In the context of implementing language features such as auto-completions, rename, references, and diagnostics, it is necessary to keep the sources up to date with the sequence of edits applied for the initial version of a given document. The Language Server Protocol has defined a set of text synchronization operations to keep the source changes up to date with the subsequent changes applied to the source files. It is important to know that all the workspace changes are not handled by the text synchronization operations. For example, let's consider that the user adds a new folder to the workspace. Such changes are notified to the server via the workspace/ didChangeWorkspaceFolders notification. In a similar manner, if the server needs to watch a specific set of files such as meta files in a project, such changes are notified with the workspace/didChangeWatchedFiles notification. We will be discussing these capabilities in Chapter 10 in detail.

---

[1] https://github.com/907th/vim-auto-save

© Nadeeshaan Gunasinghe and Nipuna Marcus 2022
N. Gunasinghe and N. Marcus, *Language Server Protocol and Implementation*,
https://doi.org/10.1007/978-1-4842-7792-8_5

General Capabilities

Even though the client must implement all three basic syncing operations (didOpen, didChange, didClose), for the server it is required to implement all three or none of the operations. In the implementation, if we have a look at the SynchronizationCapabilities class, we have access to three APIs as getWillSave, getDidSave, and getWillSaveWaitUntil. This allows the server to assume that the client implements the three basic syncing operations.

During the initialization of the server as described in Chapter 4, the server sets the capabilities for text synchronization. Language Server implementation sets the optional textDocumentSync option to configure text synchronization. Listing 5-1 shows setting the text document synchronization option in our example scenario, and Listing 5-2 shows the usage at the server's initialization.

Listing 5-1. Setting the Text Document Sync Options (ServerInitUtils.java)

```java
public static TextDocumentSyncOptions getDocumentSyncOption() {
    TextDocumentSyncOptions syncOptions =
            new TextDocumentSyncOptions();
    // set include text property to true
    SaveOptions saveOptions = new SaveOptions(true);
    // Can use Incremental for diff based approach
    // Can use None and if not set, default is None
    syncOptions.setChange(TextDocumentSyncKind.Full);
    // Client will send open and close notifications
    syncOptions.setOpenClose(true);
    syncOptions.setWillSave(true);
    syncOptions.setWillSaveWaitUntil(true);
    // With save options server can
    syncOptions.setSave(saveOptions);
    return syncOptions;
}
```

Listing 5-2. Setting the Text Document Sync Options at Initialization
(BalLanguageServer.java)

```
public CompletableFuture<InitializeResult>
            initialize(InitializeParams params) {
      return CompletableFuture.supplyAsync(() -> {
                serverContext.setClientCapabilities(params.
                getCapabilities());
                ServerCapabilities sCapabilities = new
                ServerCapabilities();
                // Set the document sync capabilities
                TextDocumentSyncOptions documentSyncOption =
                ServerInitUtils.getDocumentSyncOption();
                sCapabilities.setTextDocumentSync(documentSyncOption);
                return new InitializeResult(sCapabilities);
        });
}
```

didOpen

The client sends the textDocument/didOpen notification request to the server upon a
document open. As mentioned in the previous section, the client should implement
the didOpen notification, while the server has the freedom whether to receive the
notification or not. In Listing 5-1, we show how to register the capability and also
specify that the server wishes to receive the textDocument/didOpen and textDocument/
didClose notifications with the syncOptions.setOpenClose(true); line.

The client sends the notification with DidOpenTextDocumentParams as the input
parameters which contains the textDocument (TextDocumentItem) field specifying the
details of the opened document, and the registration options can be specified by the
server with the TextDocumentChangeRegistrationOptions data model. When the server
needs to receive didOpen notifications for custom file patterns such as a specific file
scheme, the server can use the registration options. You can refer to the initialized
method in the BalLanguageServer class to refer to the implementation of registration
options for the didOpen event on text files. The TextDocumentItem contains the
following fields.

The `textDocument.uri` field specifies the text document's URI. When we consider a compiler/parser, based on the implementation they can consider the physical file location as the source of truth, and during parsing the file content is read from the physical location. In modern parsers, this is not a common behavior, and most of the parsers allow generating an in-memory model and carry out consecutive updates on the model. The meaning of a file open can be different from a language to another. Certain programming languages and frameworks have a program structure consisting of more than a single file. For example, a Java project can contain more than one Java file and packages/modules, and also we can write a program in a single Java file. In our example implementation for Ballerina, we make use of two of the project modes, a single file project and a build project.

In both of these project modes, we are going to allow the compiler to perform the initial loading of the project from the physical location. If we look at the `didOpen` notification's parameters (`TextDocumentItem`), we get the source content of the document from the `textDocument.text`. In our implementation, we avoid processing the content at document open and use the document URI to load the project. Consider a scenario where we need to provide language intelligence for in-memory documents (untitled and unsaved), and then the server needs to initialize the project in-memory. The document content is the only source of truth in such scenarios to initialize a project.

The `textDocument.languageId` property specifies the language ID assigned for the particular document. In general, the language ID is defined by the client based on the file extension. You can refer to VS Code's language identifiers[2] as a reference and for more details.

The `textDocument.version` property specifies the version number of the document. The version number of the document will be increased for each change carried out over the document such as editing the document, undo, redo, etc. The server can utilize the version for more complex use cases such as version controlling implementations, and when it comes to incremental source updates, document versions can be used for backward referencing the changes done on a syntax tree.

---

[2] https://code.visualstudio.com/docs/languages/identifiers

Note   VS Code allows to change the language ID of an untitled/unsaved document, and language features can be provided for the particular language.

Note   Project loading depends on the compiler/parser APIs provided by the programming language. Certain APIs do not allow to generate an in-memory model, and in such scenarios, server implementations can have indexing mechanisms to avoid file I/O.

Indexing and Project Initialization

Let's consider a scenario where a user opens a document in a Ballerina project. Then in our example implementation, in Listing 5-3 we are going to initiate a new project instance upon the didOpen notification. When the request is received, we query the CompilerManager instance to access a project already built for the URI. The CompilerManager instance acts as a simplified cache/index, and once we initiate a project instance, we are going to save it in memory. If the user is going to open another document in the same project, we won't need to reinitialize a new project instance, and we can use the project instance which has been saved in memory.

Listing 5-3.   Project Initiation at didOpen (BalTextDocumentService.java)

```
public void didOpen(DidOpenTextDocumentParams params) {
    String uri = params.getTextDocument().getUri();
    Path uriPath = CommonUtils.uriToPath(uri);
    Optional<Project> projectForPath =
    this.compilerManager.getProject(uriPath);
    /*
    If the project already exists in the compiler manager that means we
    have sent the diagnostics for the project earlier. Hence we do not
    need to publish the diagnostics again. This will save a significant
    number of `publishDiagnostic` calls for projects with a many files
    */
    if (projectForPath.isEmpty()) {
        Optional<Project> project =
                this.documentSyncHandler.didOpen(params);
```

```
    project
        .ifPresent(this.diagnosticsPublisher::publish;
  }
}
```

Let's consider a developer who opens a document and needs to observe compile-time errors and warnings. These are called diagnostics, and in general, the clients show a colored squiggle under the text for various errors and warnings.

The Language Server Protocol allows the server to publish diagnostics to the client, and the client shows them with different perspectives to the users. Upon a file open notification, this is another important task we can implement. In Listing 5-3, we are publishing the diagnostics of the opened project upon the didOpen notification. We are going to compile the in-memory model and then extract all the diagnostics generated. This has been further optimized to avoid republishing the same diagnostics multiple times for multiple didOpen notifications for different documents in the same project.

didChange

The client sends the didChange notification to the server with DidChangeTextDocumentParams as the input parameters in order to notify a content change added to an opened document. The DidChangeTextDocumentParams contains the following properties.

The textDocument (VersionedTextDocumentIdentifier) property specifies the text document associated with the changes.

The contentChanges (TextDocumentContentChangeEvent) specifies the changes associated with the particular change notification.

The shape of the notification's payload differs based on the TextDocumentSyncKind set during the capability registration. There are three text synchronization variations as follows:

1. Full

2. Incremental

3. None

If the server sets the synchronization kind to None, then the client will not send any of the synchronization notifications to the server. When Full synchronization is used, the client always sends the whole document content to the server. If Incremental synchronization is used, the client sends a set of diffs to the server for each of the content changes.

Listing 5-4. Full Text Synchronization

```
Params: {
    "textDocument": {
        "uri": "file:///ls/projects/practice-concepts/main.bal",
        "version": 65
    },
    "contentChanges": [
      {
            "text": "public function main() {\n    string message =
            \"Hello World\";\n}"
      }
    ]
}
```

Listing 5-5. Incremental Text Synchronization

```
Params: {
    "textDocument": {
        "uri": "file:///ls/projects/practice-concepts/main.bal",
        "version": 8
    },
    "contentChanges": [
      {
            "range": {
                "start": {
                    "line": 1,
                    "character": 22
                },
```

```
                    "end": {
                            "line": 1,
                            "character": 27
                    }
            },
        "rangeLength": 5,
        "text": "Hello World"
      }
   ]
}
```

Listing 5-4 shows a trace extracted for `Full` text synchronization mode, where the server sends an array of text changes with the full text. Listing 5-5 shows a trace extracted for `Incremental` text synchronization mode, where the server sends an array of text changes with the text change and the range which the particular text change affected.

The incremental text mode is effective for saving bandwidth when the server is working with large text contents. When we are working with the incremental mode, it is important to evaluate the parsers' capability of handling partial text updates. When using the parsers which only can handle full text updates, the server has to have a layer to handle partial content updates before handing over the source to the parser.

In our implementation, we are going to use the full text synchronization mode since the Ballerina parser has the ability to update project models reusing existing data models.

When we consider the subsequent source edits by a user, these source changes introduce incomplete source codes which leads to semantic and syntactic errors. For example, a user removing a semicolon can introduce a syntax error, while a variable name change can lead to semantic errors. During these subsequent changes, the user should be able to see the diagnostics on the client/tool. In order to provide more accurate and up-to-date diagnostics, the server implementation can publish diagnostics upon the receiving of `didChange` notification as we demonstrated in `didOpen` notification processing.

Listing 5-6. Handling didChange Event (BalTextDocumentService.java)

```
public void didChange(DidChangeTextDocumentParams params) {
      Optional<Project> project =
               this.documentSyncHandler.didChange(params);
      Path pathUri = CommonUtils.uriToPath(params.getTextDocument().getUri());
      /*
```

```
      Publish the diagnostics upon the changes of the document.
      Even this is a single file change, the semantics can
      affect the whole project. Therefore we have to publish
      the diagnostics for the whole project.
      */
      project.ifPresent(prj -> context.diagnosticPublisher().
      publish(context, pathUri));
}
```

The registration options for the didChange event has been specified with TextDocumentChangeRegistrationOptions which contains the syncKind (TextDocumentSyncKind) property which we discussed earlier as well as the properties which we discussed for the didOpen notification's registration options.

Note   Server implementation can vary depending on the time consumed by the compiler and the parser to generate the diagnostics. In some cases, we can use debouncing approaches as well to publish diagnostics.

---

willSave

The textDocument/willSave notification is sent from the client to the server before saving the document. As mentioned earlier in this chapter, the server can access the willSave client capability via the SynchronizationCapabilities API. Also, the server can register the capability for willSave as shown in Listing 5-1.

The client sends the WillSaveTextDocumentParams with the notification, and the reason property specifies the cause for saving the document. Currently, three options are supported as Manual, AfterDelay, and FocusOut. In cases where the client is configured not to auto-save the source, then the user manually saves the document. In this scenario, the client sets the reason to Manual. In the auto-save scenario, the client sets the reason to AfterDelay. In some scenarios, the client saves the document when the editor goes out of focus, and then the reason will be set to FocusOut.

The registration options for the willSave operation are specified with TextDocumentRegistrationOptions as in the didOpen operation.

The server can carry out various tasks upon the document save. One of the common tasks is generating/dumping the logs. In such scenarios, the server has to check the reason since in auto-save mode the frequency notification is higher than the manual document save mode. Depending on the task to be carried out and the computation time required, the server can decide in which mode the server needs to carry out the operation.

willSaveWaitUntil

The client sends the `textDocument/willSaveWaitUntil` request to the server before saving the actual document and waits for any `TextEdits` and applies them before saving the document.

Consider the use case of adding a new line at the end of each document unless the document ends with a new line. Also, scenarios such as formatting the source on saving can be carried out even if the client does not support `onSaveFormatting` capability.

As mentioned earlier in this chapter, the server can access the `willSaveWaitUntil` client capability via the `SynchronizationCapabilities` API. Also, the server can register the capability for `willSaveWaitUntil` as shown in Listing 5-1.

The client sends the `WillSaveTextDocumentParams` with the request, and as in the `willSave` notification, the reason property specifies the cause of the file save operation. As a response, the server sends an array of `TextEdits`, and the clients might drop the returned `TextEdits` if the response takes a considerable time to complete. This way the clients can ensure faster document saving without interrupting the developer experience.

The registration options for the `willSaveWaitUntil` operation are specified with `TextDocumentRegistrationOptions` as in the `didOpen` operation.

Listing 5-7 shows adding a new line on the `willSaveWaitUntil` request.

Listing 5-7. Add Ending New Line on the willSaveWaitUntil Request (BalTextDocumentService.java)

```
public CompletableFuture<List<TextEdit>>
willSaveWaitUntil(WillSaveTextDocumentParams params) {
    return CompletableFuture.supplyAsync(() -> {
      BaseOperationContext context =
          ContextBuilder.baseContext(this.serverContext);
      ClientCapabilities clientCapabilities =
```

```
        this.serverContext.getClientCapabilities().orElseThrow();
    if (!clientCapabilities.getTextDocument()
        .getSynchronization().getWillSaveWaitUntil()) {
      return null;
    }
    // Here we do not consider the reason property
    String uri = params.getTextDocument().getUri();
    Path path = CommonUtils.uriToPath(uri);
    Optional<TextEdit> textEdit =
        TextModifierUtil.withEndingNewLine(path, context);

    return textEdit
        .map(Collections::singletonList)
        .orElse(Collections.emptyList());
  });
}
```

didSave

The client sends the textDocument/didSave notification to the server when the document is saved. As shown in Listing 5-1, the server can initiate whether to include the saved document content with the notification (SaveOptions). It is not always a must for the client to support this notification, and also the server can specify whether to receive this notification or not. If the server is supposed to carry out an operation on top of the document content, then it is better to include the content with the notification's parameters. Otherwise, it will save bandwidth by avoiding including the source content. Also, the registration options are specified with TextDocumentSaveRegistrationOptions which includes the includeText property. If the server sets the includeText property, the client will include the text content of the document along with the notification's input parameters.

The client sends the textDocument/didSave notification with the DidSaveTextDocumentParams which includes the following properties.

The textDocument property specifies the text document associated with the save event and represented with TextDocumentIdentifier.

The text property specifies the text content on the document when saving. This field will be populated only when the server specifies to include the content with the SaveOptions as mentioned earlier.

Note   The frequency of the didSave notification is lesser than the didChange notification. Therefore, for gaining better performance for operations such indexing, caching, and publishing the diagnostics, the server can rely on the didSave notification. However, there are exceptions as well.

---

didClose

The client sends the textDocument/didClose notification to the server when the client closes a document. The registration options for the notification are specified with the TextDocumentRegistrationOptions data model as we discussed in the didOpen notification. In Listing 5-1, we specify that the server wishes to receive the open and close notifications. The client sends the DidCloseTextDocumentParams, and it contains the textDocument to identify the particular document. After the client sends the didClose notification, the server can handle post notification tasks such as clearing internal caches and indexes. In our example scenario, we maintain two modes of projects as single file projects and multi-module projects with multiple files. Once the client closes a document which is a single file project, we are going to remove it from the internal project cache in order to avoid growing the cache. Listing 5-8 shows the cached item removal.

Listing 5-8. Remove Project from Cache on didClose (BaseDocumentSyncHandler.java)

```
public void didClose(DidCloseTextDocumentParams params,
BaseOperationContext context) {
        String uri = params.getTextDocument().getUri();
        Path path = CommonUtils.uriToPath(uri);
        CompilerManager compilerManager = context.compilerManager();
        Project project = compilerManager.getProject(path).orElseThrow();
        // Remove the project only if a single file project
```

```
if (project.kind() == ProjectKind.SINGLE_FILE_PROJECT) {
    this.compilerManager.invalidate(path);
}
}
```

> **Note**   The registration options can be used to register the server capabilities dynamically, and also they leverage the ability for the servers to bind the capabilities for multiple document selectors. For example, the server can register the **didOpen** capability for .bal sources as well as .txt sources. Once the registration is done, the server will receive didOpen notifications for both .bal sources and .txt sources.

Summary

In this chapter, we had a look at the different text synchronization methods available in the Language Server Protocol. Server implementations should pay a great deal of focus on text synchronization because the syntax and semantic states of sources depend on the valid and up-to-date versions of the given text documents. Depending on parser and compiler behaviors and capabilities, maintaining the source of truth can be varied. In case the parsers cannot maintain in-memory models, then the source of truth will always be the document in the disk. In order to avoid excessive disk access, the server implementation will have to implement a proper caching or indexing mechanism.

The server can improve the performance by utilizing synchronization capabilities such as incremental updates. Also, use cases such as diagnostics publishing can also be carried out in combination with text synchronization operations. When it comes to the server implementation, there are no standard implementation combinations of synchronization capabilities. For example, certain server implementations can ignore open and close notifications and can only depend on document change notifications. The combination of document save operations along with document change notifications allows the servers to implement more advanced use cases such as intelligent cache eviction policies and more. Once document changes are synchronized, the server can facilitate language features for up-to-date sources. In the next chapter, we are going to look at one of the most important sets of language features provided by the Language Server Protocol to facilitate publishing diagnostics, smart editing, and documentation.

CHAPTER 6

Diagnostics, Smart Editing, and Documentation

In this chapter, we will be looking at some important aspects in source code editing and how they have been addressed in a Language Server implementation. In Chapter 5, we had a brief look at the diagnostics and how to publish them. In this chapter, we will look at the diagnostics in detail. For smart editing experience, language features such as auto-completion and signature help are essential. Also, when executing language features such as auto-completion and signature help, proper documentation makes the experience a more rich experience. Language features such as hover are more frequently used by the developers to quickly access the symbol information (documentation, typing, etc.).

Diagnostics

Initialization and Capabilities

During source editing, it is important for a developer to be aware of various errors and warnings in the source code. Mainly, these errors and warnings are generated by a compiler. For example, we can consider syntax errors such as missing tokens and semantic errors such as redeclared symbol errors. Other than these errors, today it has become a key requirement to provide linting errors, warnings, and compiler-generated hints for best practices. For some languages and platforms, such tools are embedded by default, while for other cases, such tools can be added as plugins or extensions for the platform.

© Nadeeshaan Gunasinghe and Nipuna Marcus 2022
N. Gunasinghe and N. Marcus, *Language Server Protocol and Implementation*,
https://doi.org/10.1007/978-1-4842-7792-8_6

The Language Server Protocol defines the publish diagnostics notification which is sent from the server to the client. A server implementation can gather diagnostics such as compiler errors and warnings for source files and send them to the client. Then the client upon receiving the notification displays the diagnostics in the user interface. Figure 6-1 is an example of how VS Code uses different approaches to visualize the diagnostics on its user interface.

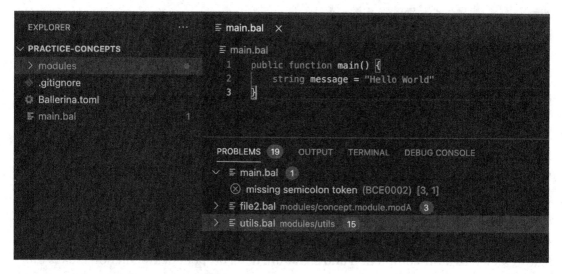

Figure 6-1. *Different forms of showing diagnostics in VS Code*

In the Language Server implementation, we can use not only the compiler-generated diagnostics but also we can integrate other tools to capture various diagnostics such as linting errors and warnings. The `PublishDiagnosticsClientCapabilities` contains the following set of properties.

The `relatedInformation` property which notifies that the client supports/accepts the related information associated with a diagnostic. For example, when the compiler complains about an error for a redeclared symbol in a given scope, then with the related information the server can specify the location of the duplicated field. We will see the example implementation and the client representation for this use case later in this section.

The `tagSupport` field specifies whether the client supports the diagnostic tags, and when the server sends an unknown tag, the client handles them gracefully. In the current implementation, the supported tags are `Unnecessary` and `Deprecated` tags. Diagnostics tagged as `Unnecessary` will be shown in faded color usually in the client's user interface. When the `Deprecated` tag is used, the diagnostic range usually will be struck through.

When the server sets the tags for the diagnostics, it is important to be aware of the set of tags supported by the client. This set of tags is sent by the client at the initialization.

The versionSupport field is set by the client when it supports the text document version associated with the diagnostic. When the server publishes the diagnostics, it can set the text document version to specify which version of the text document is associated with the particular diagnostic.

The codeDescriptionSupport specifies whether the client supports the diagnostics to set a description for the particular diagnostic code.

The dataSupport property specifies whether the client allows to set additional data with the diagnostics. When the server sets the data with the diagnostics, the data will be preserved when the client sends the textDocument/codeAction request. We will be discussing this usage more in the "Code Actions" section in Chapter 7.

Listing 6-1 shows a trace for PublishDiagnosticsClientCapabilities extracted from the client's initialize request.

Listing 6-1. Extracted Trace for the Client's Diagnostic Capabilities

```
"textDocument": {
    "publishDiagnostics": {
        "relatedInformation": true,
        "versionSupport": false,
        "tagSupport": {
            "valueSet": [1,2]
        },
        "codeDescriptionSupport": true,
        "dataSupport": true
    }
}
```

Publishing the Diagnostics

Listing 6-2 shows an example use case where we publish the diagnostics to the client when the server receives the didOpen notification. The Language Server implementation captures the compiler-generated diagnostics and publishes them as it is.

Listing 6-2. Publish Compiler-Generated Diagnostics

```
Params: {
    "uri": "file://...",
    "diagnostics": [
      {
        "range": {
          "start": {
            "line": 1,
            "character": 4
          },
          "end": {
            "line": 1,
            "character": 31
          }
        },
        "severity": 1,
        "code": "BCE2000",
        "message": "undefined module 'io'",
        "tags": []
      }
    ]
}
```

Note   In general, there are different ways the diagnostics can be generated for a given source. By default, compilers generate diagnostics for semantic and syntax incompatibilities according to the language specification and the grammar.

Other than that, there can be compiler plugins such as linters as well as code sniffers which generate the diagnostics. Even the server implementation can do code analysis and generate plugin-specific diagnostics and publish via the Language Server Protocol.

In our example, the line range is extracted from the compiler's diagnostics as well as the severity. According to the specification, the severity is not mandatory to set from the server, and when this happens, it's the client's responsibility to derive the severity from the diagnostic. Even though the client can handle the severity gracefully in such scenarios, properly addressing the severity at the server level would be ideal since all the necessary information such as compiler knowledge is available at the server implementation. Compilers generally assign a diagnostic code for a given diagnostic. Sometimes, diagnostic codes can be grouped for a set of common diagnostics and sometimes can be unique for each diagnostic. Setting the diagnostic code is optional when publishing the diagnostics.

Diagnostic source can be specified when creating the diagnostics. Even though the particular property is an optional property, it is important when collecting diagnostics from multiple sources. As mentioned earlier, diagnostics can be generated not only from the compiler but also via other tools such as linters. Linters analyze the source code for various programmatic errors other than the errors generated by the compiler itself. These include security issues, styling issues, potential bugs, and many others. In general, the linting phase is a time-consuming phase, and when it comes to the actual source editing experience, it is not necessary to publish such linting diagnostics at the same time. Since the Language Server Protocol has defined the diagnostic publishing as a notification initiated by the server, this particular use case can be handled by the server without affecting the user experience. Listing 6-3 shows how the server is using a sample linter to capture unused function diagnostics and publishing them along with compiler-generated diagnostics.

Listing 6-3. Extracted Trace for the Client's Diagnostic Capabilities (DiagnosticsPublisherImpl.java)

```java
public void publish(BaseOperationContext context, Path path) {
    Optional<Project> project =
            context.compilerManager().getProject(path);
    if (project.isEmpty()) {
        return;
    }
    DiagnosticResult diagResult = project.get().currentPackage()
            .getCompilation().diagnosticResult();
    Map<String, List<Diagnostic>> diagnostics = new HashMap<>();
    // Get the compiler generated diagnostics
    List<io.ballerina.tools.diagnostics.Diagnostic>
            allDiagnostics = new ArrayList<>(diagResult.diagnostics());
    // Get the diagnostics from the linter
    allDiagnostics.addAll(BallerinaLinter
```

```
            .getFunctionDiagnostics(path, context));
    allDiagnostics.addAll(BallerinaLinter
            .getRedeclaredVarDiagnostics(path, context));
    // Fill the diagnostics to the return list
    allDiagnostics.forEach(diagnostic -> {
        String diagPath = diagnostic.location().lineRange().filePath();
        Diagnostic computedDiag = this.getDiagnostic(diagnostic);
        List<DiagnosticTag> tags = new ArrayList<>();
        if (diagnostic.diagnosticInfo().code().
        equals(LinterDiagnosticCodes.LINTER001.getDiagnosticCode())) {
            tags.add(DiagnosticTag.Unnecessary);
        }
        if (diagnostic.diagnosticInfo().code().
        equals(LinterDiagnosticCodes.LINTER002.getDiagnosticCode())) {
            tags.add(DiagnosticTag.Deprecated);
        }
        computedDiag.setTags(tags);
        if (diagnostic instanceof RedeclaredVarDiagnostic) {
            io.ballerina.tools.diagnostics.DiagnosticRelatedInformation
            rInfo =
                    ((RedeclaredVarDiagnostic) diagnostic).
                    relatedInformation();
            DiagnosticRelatedInformation relatedInfo =
                    new DiagnosticRelatedInformation();
            relatedInfo.setMessage(rInfo.message());
            relatedInfo.setLocation(getRelatedInfoLocation(rInfo,
            project.get()));
        }
        if (diagnostics.containsKey(diagPath)) {
            diagnostics.get(diagPath).add(computedDiag);
        } else {
            List<Diagnostic> diags = new ArrayList<>();
            diagnostics.put(diagPath, diags);
        }
    });
```

```
    /*
    Go through the previously published diagnostics
    and clear the diagnostics associated with a
    particular file uri by setting an empty list.
     */
    this.previousDiagnostics.forEach((diagPath, diagnosticList) -> {
        if (!diagnostics.containsKey(diagPath)) {
            diagnostics.put(diagPath, new ArrayList<>());
        }
    });
    diagnostics.forEach((diagPath, diagList) -> {
        PublishDiagnosticsParams params =
                new PublishDiagnosticsParams();
        params.setDiagnostics(diagList);
        URI uri = project.get().sourceRoot().resolve(diagPath).toUri();
        params.setUri(uri.toString());

        this.client.publishDiagnostics(params);
    });

    this.previousDiagnostics = diagnostics;
}
```

As per the protocol, the client does not clear the diagnostics automatically. In order to clear or refresh diagnostics, the server has to specifically clear the diagnostics associated with a certain document uri. As in Listing 6-3, a call to the publish method, we go through the existing diagnostics (diagnostics published previously) and invalidate the stale diagnostics compared with the latest diagnostics.

Note   For a given server instance, we have only one diagnostic publisher, so the server can clear the previous diagnostics published for the workspace.

The diagnostic message is mandatory and shows the description of the particular error or the warning.

An optional array of DiagnosticTags can be used to specify a richer diagnostic representation for scenarios such as deprecated constructs and unused constructs.

The current protocol implementation specifies two kinds of tags as unnecessary and deprecated. In Listing 6-3, we set the diagnostic tags for linter diagnostics. Usually, the unnecessary information is visualized as faded text, while the deprecated information is struck through.

The related Information property can take an array of RelatedInformation to specify other ranges of the document affected by a certain diagnostic. Let's consider a scenario where there is a redeclared symbol. When the source code grows, it is important to highlight all occurrences of such diagnostics for a better viewpoint of the effect. With the related information, we can specify such occurrences. Listing 6-3 shows setting the related information at server implementation.

Completion

Auto-completion can be considered as one of the most crucial features for developers. Today, developers heavily depend on content assist features for a faster development experience. Content assist is not just suggesting available tokens and symbols to the developer, instead it has to be well aware of the contextual information of the current cursor position, language semantics, as well as, in the case of programming languages, the awareness about the ecosystem. We will look at how we can provide a richer content assist/auto-completion experience with the server implementation of the Language Server Protocol.

Initialization and Capabilities

When the server receives the initialize request, the client capabilities of the completion language feature can be read.

Client Capabilities

The client capabilities are specified with CompletionClientCapabilities data model. The dynamicRegistration property specifies whether the client allows the completion language feature to be registered dynamically.

The completionItem.snippetSupport property specifies whether the client can support the snippet syntax defined in the specification[1] for the completion items. Each

---

[1] https://microsoft.github.io/language-server-protocol/specifications/specification-3-16/#snippet_syntax

completion item generated is supposed to have an insert text (if not the label is used) which will be inserted to the source upon the selection of the particular completion item. In some cases, the completion item can insert a plain text token such as a keyword in the language. When suggesting smarter completions, the server can derive various language constructs in the form of snippets. For example, the user can be provided with a snippet to insert a function at the top level. In such cases, the construct can have variable value portions where the user can provide a desired value – such as the name of the function. Snippets allow the server to set such placeholders with default values, and then upon the selection of the completion item, the user can navigate through the items with the tab selection while editing the snippet.

The `completionItem.commitCharactersSupport` specifies whether the client accepts commit characters with a completion item. Consider an expression such as `studentList.<cursor>length().toString()`. When we consider the cursor position mentioned in the expression, the user can write a chained invocation having expressions separated by the `period` character. With the commit characters support, the completion item can be set with the `period` as a commit character. When the user presses the period character, the client inserts the `length()` and then the `period`.

The `completionItem.documentationFormat` is an optional property which takes an array of `MarkupKinds`. The current specification supports `plainText` and `markdown` markup kinds. When the server creates a completion item, we can set any documentation associated with the particular completion item. For example, when we consider a function definition with documentation, then the server can add the particular documentation of the function to the completion item. When the user goes through the list of completion items, the documentation is shown. The documentation in the markdown format can be used to visualize the documentation in a richer format. It is important at the server to generate the documentation analyzing this particular client capability option, in order to provide the user a better user experience. The order of the array specifies the client's preference of the markup kind when rendering in the user interface.

The `completionItem.deprecatedSupport` property specifies whether the client can support the deprecated item rendering in the completion item list. When creating a completion item, the server can set the deprecated property of the completion item, and the client can render those specially within the list. Since the deprecated field setting in the completion item is **deprecated**, it is recommended to use the **completion tags** instead. We will be discussing this with the examples later in this section.

The `completionItem.preselectSupport` field specifies whether the client can preselect a completion item. We will discuss this behavior in the next section.

The `completionItem.tagSupport` specifies whether the client supports setting the tags in completion items and specifies the list of tags supported by the client. Currently, the protocol supports the `deprecated` tag and can be used instead of the `deprecated` property in the completion item. When creating a completion item for constructs such as functions, the server can set deprecation status for the symbol. This property is useful in such scenarios. If the server needs to spend additional cycles to reveal the deprecated status, before the processing it is a better option to check for the client support with this property.

The `insertReplaceSupport` specifies whether the client allows the server to set a completion item with the capability, when selected, either to replace the text or to insert the text.

The `resolveSupport.properties` specifies an array of properties which can be resolved via the `completion/resolve` request.

The `insertTextModeSupport` specifies whether the client allows the server to configure the insert mode of whitespace characters. Currently, there are two modes defined in the Language Server specification as `adjustIndentation` and `asIs`. When it comes to snippet completions as well as multiline completions, servers can set the mode to adjust the indentation when selecting the particular completion item.

The `completionItemKind` specifies the list of item kinds supported by the client, and when specified, the client guarantees that it would handle the unknown item kinds set by the server gracefully and use a default kind for them. Item kinds are used to specify the distinction between completion items when presenting in the user interface. For example, there are various types of completion items such as for variables, types, snippets, etc. When completion items are showing in the user interface, the client can use the item kind to differentiate the entries.

The `contextSupport` specifies whether the client can send additional context information with the completion request.

Server Capabilities

Server capabilities are specified with the `CompletionOptions` data model. The server specifies the supported capabilities by setting specific properties associated with the `CompletionOptions` as we discussed next.

The `triggerCharacters` property specifies the set of characters which the server expects to trigger the completion request. In general, the clients automatically trigger the completion request upon the alphabetical characters. When it comes to language semantics, there are special characters used for various use cases. In our example use case for Ballerina, -> is used for action invocations. Therefore, in our auto-completion implementation, we expect the client to trigger the auto-completion when the user types the > character, so the server can suggest the available actions over a given client.

The allCommitCharacters property specifies the set of commit characters where the server expects to support. As described in the "Client Capabilities" section, when the client supports commit characters, then the server can set commit characters with the completion item. In case the client does not support commit characters to be set with completion items, then the allCommitCharacters can be used by the client. If the server has set both allCommitCharacters and individual commit characters in a given completion item, priority is given to commit characters set along with the completion item.

The resolveProvider property specifies whether the server supports resolving additional information associated with the completion item with the completion/ resolve request. The set of properties which can be resolved will be set by the client with the resolveSupport.properties.

Listing 6-4 shows setting the server capabilities for the textDocument/completion request.

Listing 6-4. Set Completion Server Capabilities (ServerInitUtils.java)

```
public static CompletionOptions getCompletionOptions() {
    CompletionOptions completionOptions = new CompletionOptions();
    // List of trigger characters.
    List<String> triggerCharacters = Arrays.asList(".", ">");
    completionOptions.setResolveProvider(true);
    completionOptions.setTriggerCharacters(triggerCharacters);
    completionOptions.setWorkDoneProgress(true);
    return completionOptions;
}
```

Generating the Completions

Auto-completions or content assist has become one of the most used language features by the developers who use any IDE/source editor. Therefore, it is important for tooling vendors to make the experience smoother and intuitive as much as possible. In different editors, there are different representations for the particular language feature. In the previous subsection, we had a look at the initialization and capabilities provided by the Language Server Protocol (LSP) for the auto-completion language feature. In this section, we are going to have a look at the various options we can provide along with a completion item.

The general request-response flow of the Language Server for triggering the auto-completion has two modes, where the first mode is the auto-completion is automatically triggered when characters are typed in the editor, and the second mode is when the user explicitly triggers shortcut key combinations (`ctrl + space`) in the editor. Also, you can see that the client notifies how the completion operation triggered with the completion context information, which we will be looking at later in this section.

When we consider the first mode, the `textDocument/didChange` notification is sent by the client to notify the character insertion. Then the client sends the `textDocument/completion` request. In order to provide reliable and up-to-date information, the server implementation has to first update the actual source/in-memory copy and then compute the completion items on those particular sources. Updating sources and invoking the particular compiler or parser depend on the underlying language's compiler implementation. If the respective compilers allow to maintain in-memory models with incremental updates, then the Language Server implementation can maintain in-memory representations to compute the completions as well. In our Language Server implementation, we are going to maintain an in-memory project cache and incrementally update sources upon `textDocument/didChange` events via the provided compiler and project APIs of the Ballerina language.

Listing 6-5 shows generating auto-completions for the function body block.

Listing 6-5. Function Body Completion Provider

```
public class FunctionBodyNodeContextProvider extends
      BalCompletionProviderImpl<FunctionBodyBlockNode> {
   @Override
   public List<CompletionItem>
   getCompletions(FunctionBodyBlockNode node,
               BalCompletionContext context) {
        List<CompletionItem> completionItems = new ArrayList<>();
      List<Symbol> symbols = context.visibleSymbols().stream()
            .filter(s -> s.kind() == SymbolKind.TYPE_DEFINITION
                  || s.kind() == SymbolKind.VARIABLE
```

```
                || s.kind() == SymbolKind.CONSTANT
                || s.kind() ==SymbolKind.FUNCTION)
            .collect(Collectors.toList());

        completionItems.addAll(this.convert(symbols, context));
        completionItems.addAll(this.getFunctionBodySnippets(context))
        return completionItems;
    }
    ...
    private List<CompletionItem>
    getFunctionBodySnippets(BalCompletionContext context) {
        return Arrays.asList(
            StatementCompletionItem.IF_BLOCK.get(context),
            StatementCompletionItem.WHILE_BLOCK.get(context)
        );
    }
}
// The Convert method resides in BalCompletionProviderImpl.
protected List<CompletionItem> convert(List<? extends Symbol> symbols,
                                    BalCompletionContext context) {
        List<CompletionItem> completionItems = new ArrayList<>();
        for (Symbol symbol : symbols) {
            if (symbol.getName().isEmpty()) {
                continue;
            }
            CompletionItem cItem = new CompletionItem();
            // Set the insert text and the label
            this.setInsertText(symbol, context, cItem);
            cItem.setLabel(symbol.getName().get());
            this.setDocumentation(symbol, context, cItem);
            this.setTags(symbol, context, cItem);
            completionItems.add(cItem);
        }

        return completionItems;
    }
```

Text Insertion

The response of the completion request is a `CompletionItem`. In our initial example in Listing 6-5, you can see that we call a method called convert which resides in the parent class `BalCompletionProviderImpl`. Here, we convert a given symbol to an associated completion item. At the end of Listing 6-5, we have shown the convert method's context where you can see that we set both the insertText and the label. When running the sample, you can observe the behavior difference of setting the insertText by commenting the `this.setInsertText(symbol, context, cItem);` line. The `label` is shown on the UI, and upon the selection of the completion item, the `label` is inserted if the `insertText` or `textEdit` is not set. The label can just contain a plain text, and in some cases, labels can be an alias for a snippet. For example, the user can provide a function snippet at the top level which will insert a function skeleton, and the label can be func which is an alias. In order to provide a better developer experience, it is a good practice to use both the label for naming the completion item and insertText or textEdit for the actual content to be added upon the completion item selection. Both `insertText` and `textEdit` are treated differently by the client's implementations.

Listing 6-6 is an example of adding snippet completion items for control flow constructs. Here, we use an enum to hold the control flow and other statement constructs. The enum takes a StatementBlock construct as the argument which holds the label, plain text–formatted insert text, and snippet-formatted insert text. We will not dig deep into this data model, and instead we will have a look at the get method which generates the completion item for the statement block.

Listing 6-6. Generate Snippets

```
public enum StatementCompletionItem {
    IF_BLOCK(StatementCompletionItemBuilder.getIfStatement()),
    WHILE_BLOCK(StatementCompletionItemBuilder.getWhileStatement());
    ...
    private final StatementCompletionItemBuilder.StatementBlock
    statementBlock;

    StatementCompletionItem(StatementCompletionItemBuilder.StatementBlock
    statementBlock) {
        this.statementBlock = statementBlock;
    }
```

```
CompletionItem get(BalCompletionContext context) {
    boolean snippetSupport = context.clientCapabilities().
    getTextDocument()
            .getCompletion().getCompletionItem().getSnippetSupport();
    CompletionItem item = new CompletionItem();
    if (snippetSupport) {
        item.setInsertText(this.statementBlock.getSnippet());
        item.setInsertTextFormat(InsertTextFormat.Snippet);
    } else {
        item.setInsertText(this.statementBlock.getPlainText());
        item.setInsertTextFormat(InsertTextFormat.PlainText);
    }
    item.setLabel(this.statementBlock.getLabel());

    return item;
    }
}
```

Earlier, we discussed that all the clients might not support the snippet-formatted insert text, and therefore the `CompletionClientCapabilities` specifies the particular support. You can see that before setting the insert text, we check whether the client supports the snippet format. By setting the insert text format, the server emphasizes to the client that the content to be inserted adheres to the snippet syntax and hence allows the user to use the tab to navigate between placeholders. If the server does not set the `insertTextFormat` field, then the client assumes the format to be `InsertTextFormat.PlainText`, and upon the selection of the completion item, the insert text will be inserted as it is. As described in the "Initialization and Capabilities" section, the client specifies whether it can handle the snippet format or not. Therefore, it is important to set the insert text in the snippet format conditionally based on the client capability.

As specified by the protocol, the client can decide how it manipulates the insert text. For example, in our use case of generating completion items for the function body in Listing 6-5, assume we capture a type definition symbol named `Person`, and when the user types `Pe` and selects `Person` from the completion item list, the VS Code client inserts `rson` to make the completed text to be `Person`. Since this might not be the behavior always, it is encouraged to use the `textEdit` field instead of the `insertText`. The `textEdit` field can hold either a `TextEdit` or an `InsertReplaceTextEdit` construct.

If the server wishes to insert a content, then the TextEdit will be the proper approach. In scenarios where the server needs to replace a certain text range with the given code content of the completion item, then the InsertReplaceEdit can be used. Listing 6-7 shows the usage of the textEdit field. If the server sets both insertText and textEdit fields, the textEdit field would be given the priority. You can see in BalCompletionProviderImpl, we have the convert method where we convert a symbol to a completion item. Listing 6-7 shows the utility method setTextEdit where we set the textEdit for the completion item. You can enable setting the insertText or textEdit by enabling either the setInsertText or the setTextEdit method.

Listing 6-7. Set textEdits for the Snippet (BalCompletionProviderImpl.java)

```
private void setTextEdit(Symbol symbol, BalCompletionContext context,
CompletionItem cItem) {
    CompletionItemCapabilities capabilities =
            context.clientCapabilities().getTextDocument()
                .getCompletion().getCompletionItem();
    StringBuilder insertTxtBuilder =
            new StringBuilder(symbol.getName().get());
    InsertTextFormat insertTextFormat;
    TextEdit textEdit = new TextEdit();
    Range range;
    NonTerminalNode nodeAtCursor = context.getNodeAtCursor();
    if (nodeAtCursor.kind() == SyntaxKind.SIMPLE_NAME_REFERENCE) {
        LineRange lineRange = ((SimpleNameReferenceNode) nodeAtCursor).
        name().lineRange();
        range = this.toRange(lineRange);
    } else {
        range = new Range(context.getCursorPosition(),
                context.getCursorPosition());
    }

    if (symbol.kind() == SymbolKind.FUNCTION) {
        insertTxtBuilder.append("(");
        Optional<List<ParameterSymbol>> params =
                ((FunctionSymbol) symbol).typeDescriptor().params();
```

```
        if (params.isPresent() && !params.get().isEmpty()
                && capabilities.getSnippetSupport()) {
            insertTxtBuilder.append("${1}");
            insertTextFormat = InsertTextFormat.Snippet;
        } else {
            insertTextFormat = InsertTextFormat.PlainText;
        }
        insertTxtBuilder.append(")");
    } else {
        insertTextFormat = InsertTextFormat.PlainText;
    }

    textEdit.setNewText(insertTxtBuilder.toString());
    textEdit.setRange(range);
    cItem.setTextEdit(Either.forLeft(textEdit));
    cItem.setInsertTextFormat(insertTextFormat);
}
```

Listing 6-8 shows the usage of InsertReplaceTextEdit. It is important that the server check the client capability before setting this particular text edit variation. It is a common scenario that the users invoke the completion in the middle of a token and want to replace the complete token. For example, in the say<cursor>Hello(); line, if the user invokes completions, it should be possible to replace the sayHello token with sayWelcome upon the selection of the sayWelcome completion item. InsertReplaceTextEdit contains two ranges, the insert range and replace range. The insert range is applied if the user asks for the insertion for the completion item, and the replace range is applied if the user asks for replacement for the completion item. If we consider our example use case, the following two behaviors will be available for the insert and replace cases, respectively:

- say<cursor>Hello - (insert) => sayWelcomeHello

- say<cursor>Hello - (replace) => sayWelcome

It is a must that the insert range be a prefix of the replace range.

Listing 6-8. Set the InsertReplaceTextEdit (BalCompletionProviderImpl.java)

```
private void setInsertReplaceTextEdit(Symbol symbol,
BalCompletionContext context, CompletionItem cItem) {
    ...
    if (nodeAtCursor.kind() == SyntaxKind.SIMPLE_NAME_REFERENCE) {
        LineRange lineRange =
                ((SimpleNameReferenceNode) nodeAtCursor).name().
                lineRange();
        Position insertStart =
                this.toPosition(lineRange.startLine());
        Position insertEnd =
                new Position(insertStart.getLine(), cursor.getCharacter());
        insertRange = new Range(insertStart, insertEnd);
        replaceRange = this.toRange(lineRange);
        // Insert range is a prefix of replace range
        InsertReplaceEdit textEdit = new InsertReplaceEdit();
        textEdit.setNewText(insertTxtBuilder.toString());
        textEdit.setInsert(insertRange);
        textEdit.setReplace(replaceRange);
        cItem.setTextEdit(Either.forRight(textEdit));
    } else {
        cItem.setInsertText(insertTxtBuilder.toString());
    }
}
```

The `additionalTextEdits` field allows the server to add further text edits to the source other than the `insertText` or `textEdit` fields' content. One such use case is to add import statements automatically upon the selection of a text edit. In our example in Listing 6-9, we are going to provide a snippet for a main function which has a print statement. This snippet will add an import statement for the `ballerina/ io` module upon the selection of the completion item. In our example use case, if the cursor is at the top level, we provide a main function snippet. Listing 6-9 is extracted from the `ModulePartNodeContextProvider` class, and you can have a look at the full implementation there.

Listing 6-9. Set Additional Text Edits

```
private CompletionItem
getMainFunctionSnippet(BalCompletionContext context) {
    String ioModuleOrg = "ballerina";
    String ioModuleAlias = "io";
    CompletionItem item = new CompletionItem();
    // The main function template
    String template = "public function main() {" + lineSeparator
            + "\tio:println(\"Hello World!!\");"
            + lineSeparator + "}";
    item.setInsertText(template);
    item.setLabel("main function");
    SyntaxTree syntaxTree = context.compilerManager()
            .getSyntaxTree(context.getPath()).orElseThrow();
    if (!TextEditGenerator.isModuleImported(ioModuleOrg,
            ioModuleAlias, syntaxTree)) {
        /*
        Range starts from the last import statement if there are
        other imports, otherwise 0,0 is chosen
         */
        Range range = getAutoImportRange(context);

        TextEdit autoImport =
                getAutoImportTextEdit("ballerina", "io", range);
        item.setAdditionalTextEdits(
                Collections.singletonList(autoImport));
        item.setKind(CompletionItemKind.Snippet);
    }
    item.setFilterText("main");

    return item;
}
```

The `insertTextMode` has been introduced to handle the indentation when inserting multiline insert text. For example, when we are inserting snippets, it is a more common requirement to have multiline snippets to include block constructs such as functions. Setting the `insertTextMode` allows the server to specify whether to use the snippet as it is (`asIs`) mode or allow it to adjust the indentation by the client (`adjustIndentation`).

Documentation and Additional Information

A completion item defines a set of fields to provide additional information to the developer. When we consider a completion item in general, the two main fields that come to our mind are the insert text and the label when in some cases both take the same value. However, we can provide the user with more information, such as details about a function (doc comments), type information of a variable, and so on. In this section, we will be looking at such capabilities we can achieve with the completion item.

The `detail` field is used to provide additional information associated with the particular completion item. For example, when we generate completion items for variables and functions, it is important to show the user the type information of variables as well as the return type information of functions. Setting the `detail` field, the server can add this information to the completion item, and this will be presented to the developer as shown in Figure 6-2.

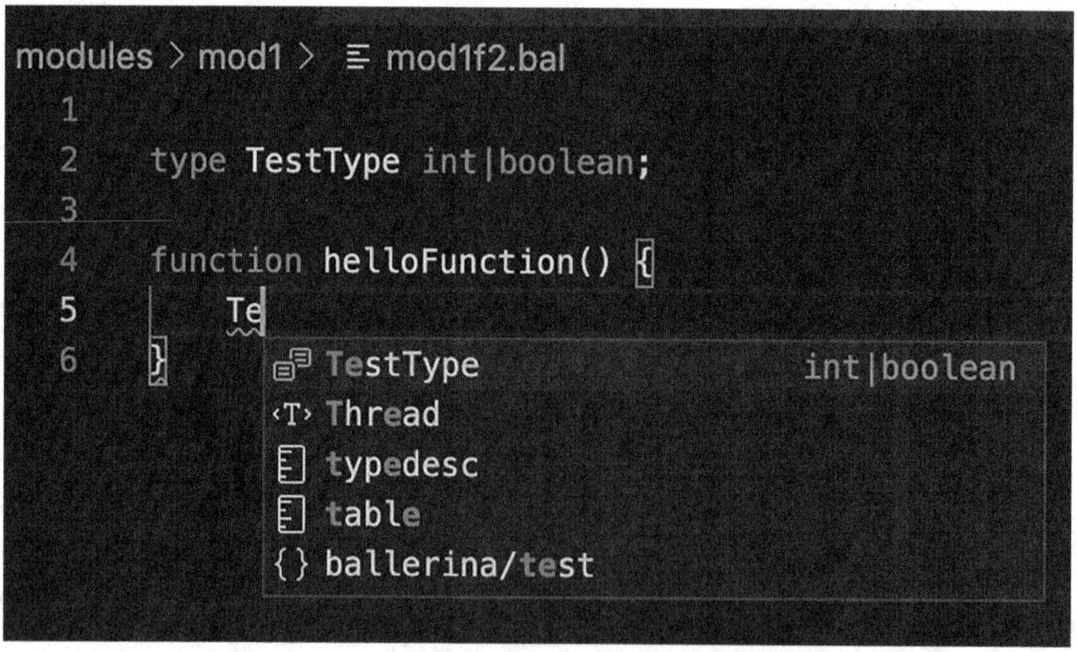

Figure 6-2. *Completion items showing the detail set by the server*

In most of the client implementations, the common practice is to show this information side by side with the label information which allows the developer to grasp the information at first glance. Figure 6-2 shows the label of the TestType type definition on the IntelliSense and int|boolean as the detail – which is the type of the particular type definition. Listing 6-10 shows setting the type signature as the detail.

The documentation field can be set to provide more descriptive information of a completion item. Documentation is more important for symbols such as functions. For example, when developers are going through the completion items, such as functions, it is a common practice to go through the documentation to get more information about the behavior of the function, input parameter details, return type details, etc. The server can set this information with the documentation field. The documentation field accepts either a plain string or a MarkupContent. Using the markup content allows the server to arrange the documentation content neatly and can provide the users a better experience. We are going to set the documentation with the completionItem/resolve request in the next section.

Listing 6-10. Set the Detail for the Completion Item (BalCompletionProviderImpl.java)

```
private void setDetail(Symbol symbol,
                       BalCompletionContext context,
                       CompletionItem cItem) {
    String detail;
    switch (symbol.kind()) {
        case FUNCTION:
            Optional<TypeSymbol> tSymbol =
                    ((FunctionSymbol) symbol).typeDescriptor()
                            .returnTypeDescriptor();
            detail = tSymbol.isPresent() ? tSymbol.get().signature() : "()";
            break;
        case TYPE_DEFINITION:
            detail = ((TypeDefinitionSymbol) symbol).typeDescriptor().
            signature();
            break;
        case VARIABLE:
            detail = ((VariableSymbol) symbol).typeDescriptor().signature();
            break;
```

```
        default:
            return;
    }

    cItem.setDetail(detail);
}
```

Note   The approach of extracting the documentation from symbols depends on the compiler APIs. In certain scenarios, the time taken to compute the documentation can affect the developer experience. In order to avoid this, the server can make use of the textDocument/completion/resolve method defined in the protocol.

The tags field allows you to add additional information when rendering the completion item in the editor. Currently, the protocol supports only one tag – the deprecated tag. Listing 6-11 shows setting the deprecated tag when the deprecated annotation has been added to the function. In BalCompletionProviderImpl, we have the setTags method which will be called within the convert function which we discussed earlier as well. Here, we check whether the top-level nodes such as functions, type definitions, and enums have the deprecated annotation added. In order to check the behavior, add a Ballerina function and then add the @deprecated annotation before the function keyword. When suggesting such a function as a completion item, the particular entry will be shown as strikethrough.

Listing 6-11. Set the Deprecated Tag for Completion Items (BalCompletionProviderImpl.java)

```
private void setTags(Symbol symbol,
                     BalCompletionContext context,
                     CompletionItem cItem) {
    List<AnnotationSymbol> annotations;
    switch (symbol.kind()) {
        case CLASS:
            annotations = ((ClassSymbol) symbol).annotations();
            break;
        case FUNCTION:
            annotations = ((FunctionSymbol) symbol).annotations();
            break;
```

```
        case TYPE_DEFINITION:
            annotations = ((TypeDefinitionSymbol) symbol).annotations();
            break;
        default:
            annotations = Collections.emptyList();
            break;
    }
    CompletionItemCapabilities itemCapabilities =
            context.clientCapabilities().getTextDocument()
                .getCompletion().getCompletionItem();
    CompletionItemTagSupportCapabilities tagSupport =
            itemCapabilities.getTagSupport();
    List<CompletionItemTag> supportedTags = tagSupport.getValueSet();

    Optional<AnnotationSymbol> deprecatedAnnotation = annotations.stream()
            .filter(annot -> annot.getName().orElse("").equals("deprecated"))
            .findAny();

    if (deprecatedAnnotation.isPresent() &&
            supportedTags.contains(CompletionItemTag.Deprecated)) {
        cItem.setTags(Collections.singletonList(CompletionItemTag.
        Deprecated));
    }
}
```

The data field is a special field which preserves the content between completion and completionItem/resolve requests. We will be looking at the behavior of this field in the "Completion Resolve" section.

The preselect option allows the server to specify what item is to be selected by default from the list of available completion items. The preselect option is a very helpful option to be used when the server can define what would be the default selection depending on various heuristics. Consider the source snippet in Listing 6-12.

Listing 6-12. Cursor position where preselect option is important

```
function sayHello(int userId) returns string {
    return "Hello! " + userId.<cursor>
}
```

At the given cursor position, the server can suggest available methods (langlib method) over the userId variable. Among them, we have the toString method which converts the userId variable to a string. By analyzing the function's signature and the return statement, the server can deduce that the user has a better chance of using the toString method, among others. In this scenario, the server can set the preselect flag for the toString completion item.

Also, it is important to keep in mind that we can set the `preselect` option to only one completion item among a list of completion items. Otherwise, the client will decide which item to be selected.

Sorting and Filtering

The `sortText` can be set to specify the order of completion items appearing in the user interface. Depending on the context where completions are triggered, the priority of completion items can be different. For example, if the user is at the top level, then it can be a frequent usage of completions to add top-level construct snippets such as function definitions, type definitions, and related definitions. If the user is within a function body, then content such as types are used frequently since the user tends to write variable definition statements and related statements more than other statements. In such scenarios, the user can collectively set the sort text of a certain element kind's completion items to appear before another element kind.

When a set of completion items shares the same sort text, the order among the set would be determined upon the label of the completion item. If the server does not set the sort text of a completion item, then the order would be determined by the `label` of the completion item. Listing 6-13 specifies the completion item sorting done for top-level constructs. In the implementation, each context has a specific completion provider, and the particular context should override the `sort` method. Once completion items are generated, the list is passed to the sort API in order to sort the generated completion items. For convenience, depending on the usage and requirements different APIs can be added for sorting completion items.

In our example use case, we are going to use the `CompletionItemKind` set for completion items to sort them. Setting the kind of a completion item is important for improving the developer experience by allowing the developer to visually group similar items.

Listing 6-13. Set Sort Text for Completion Items
(ModulePartNodeContextProvider.java)

```
public void sort(ModulePartNode node, BalCompletionContext context,
List<CompletionItem> items) {
    items.forEach(completionItem -> {
        if (completionItem.getKind()== CompletionItemKind.Snippet) {
            // Snippets are given the highest priority
            completionItem.setSortText("A");
        } else {
            completionItem.setSortText("B");
        }
    });
}
```

The `filterText` can be set to specify which text should be used to filter the given completion item. By default, the `label` is used and highlighted while filtering the completion item list. When we set the `filterText` even though the filter text is not visible, these items will appear in the completion item list. This is again valuable for grouping completion items and also for assigning aliases for completion items. Consider our sample in Listing 6-9 where we create a snippet for the main function. The label we set for the main function is `public main function`, which is behaving inconsistently when filtering. Hence, we set `main` as the filter text for the particular completion item.

Completion Resolve

The `completionItem/resolve` request is sent from the client to the server to request additional information for a completion item. A `CompletionItem` is the request parameter, and as a response, the server sends back a `CompletionItem`. In general, certain information associated with a given completion item can be impacted to the response time of the `textDocument/completion` request. The resolving of these additional information depends on the compilers'/ parsers' behavior. For example, if the compiler takes a significant time to compose the documentation associated with symbols, then the server can generate completion items without the documentation field, and then upon the resolve request, the server can capture the documentation and enrich the completion item. As mentioned in the previous section, the `data` field of a completion item is preserved during `completion` and `completionItem/resolve` requests. If the server needs metadata to proceed with the `completionItem/resolve` request, then the data field can be used to pass the data between these two requests. Listings 6-14 and 6-15 together are an example for the aforementioned use case.

In Listing 6-9, we had a look at adding a main function template as a snippet completion item with additional text edits for an import statement. Such additional text edit generation needs extra processing of the syntax trees, and we can avoid this with the resolve request. In Listing 6-14, we are generating a new HTTP service template in the snippet format with an import statement. Also, we are not going to generate the additional text edit for the import statement which we are going to add automatically upon the selection of the completion item. Instead, we set metadata such as the document URI where the import statement should be added as well as the import statement to be added (`import ballerina/http;`). This meta-information will be wrapped with a POJO (Plain Old Java Object) for the ease of use when converting. The `AutoImportTextEditData` object will be the data model here.

As we discussed in the "Completion" section, the client capabilities specify the properties which can be lazily loaded with the resolve request. In Listing 6-14, you can see the line segment `properties.contains("additionalTextEdits")` where we check whether the client supports loading the additional text edits lazily. Currently, the VS Code client supports the documentation, detail, and `additionalTextEdits` to be loaded lazily. It is important to be mindful in the server implementation to check the supported properties before proceeding in order to avoid suggesting less information to the users.

You can observe this behavior from the client point of view by enabling trace logs in the client by setting the `"ballerina-lang-client.trace.server": "verbose"` option in VS Code user settings and invoking completions in a Ballerina source, and these particular completions will be triggered only at the top level.

Listing 6-14. Set Metadata for Service Skeleton in ModulePartNodeContextProvider

```
private CompletionItem getHttpServiceSnippet(BalCompletionContext context)
{
    CompletionItem item = new CompletionItem();
    String template = "service /${1} on new http:Listener(8080)
            {" + lineSeparator + "\tresource function ${2:get}
            ${3:getResource}"
```

```
        + "(http:Caller ${4:caller}, " + "http:Request ${5:req})
        {" + lineSeparator
        + "\t\t" + lineSeparator + "\t}" + lineSeparator + "}";
    item.setInsertText(template);
    item.setInsertTextFormat(InsertTextFormat.Snippet);
    item.setLabel("service - http");
    item.setFilterText("service");
    SyntaxTree syntaxTree = context.compilerManager()
            .getSyntaxTree(context.getPath()).orElseThrow();
    List<String> properties = context.clientCapabilities().getTextDocument()
            .getCompletion().getCompletionItem()
            .getResolveSupport().getProperties();
    String importStmt = "import ballerina/http;";
    if (properties.contains("additionalTextEdits")) {
        // proceed with resolve and set data
        String uri = context.getPath().toUri().toString();
        AutoImportTextEditData data =
            new AutoImportTextEditData(uri, importStmt);
        item.setData(data);
    } else {
        TextEdit autoImport = TextEditGenerator
            .getAutoImport(importStmt, syntaxTree);
        item.setAdditionalTextEdits(
            Collections.singletonList(autoImport));
    }

    return item;
}
```

Listing 6-15. Generate a Resolved Completion Item in the
CompletionItemResolver Utility

```
public static CompletionItem
resolve(BalCompletionResolveContext context) {
    CompletionItem unresolved = context.unresolved();
    Optional<AutoImportTextEditData> data =
            getAutoImportTextEditData(unresolved.getData());
```

```
    if (data.isEmpty()) {
        return unresolved;
    }

    // Create a clone for the unresolved CompletionItem
    CompletionItem clone = clone(unresolved);
    Path path = CommonUtils.uriToPath(data.get().getUri());
    SyntaxTree syntaxTree = context.compilerManager()
            .getSyntaxTree(path).orElseThrow();
    // Analyze the syntax tree and generate the text edit
    TextEdit textEdit = TextEditGenerator
            .getAutoImport(data.get().getImportStatement(), syntaxTree);
    clone.setAdditionalTextEdits(Collections.singletonList(textEdit));
    return clone;
}
```

Signature Help

The textDocument/signatureHelp request is sent from the client to the server requesting signature information. Signature help is used to provide parameter information about a method/function invocation construct in a given programming language or similar scripting language.

Initialization and Capabilities

Client Capabilities

Client capabilities are specified with the SignatureHelpClientCapabilities data model, where the following properties are available.

The dynamicRegistration property specifies whether the client allows the server to dynamically register and unregister the signature help capabilities where the registration options are specified with the SignatureHelpRegistrationOptions data model.

The signatureInformation.documentationFormat is as we described in the textDocument/completion request.

The `signatureInformation.parameterInformation` up to the current specification describes whether the client supports the label offset instead of the label strings. In order to highlight the parameters, the server can use either the label offset or the label string. We will be looking at this later in this section.

The `signatureInformation.activeParameterSupport` specifies whether the client allows the server to set the active parameter within the `SignatureInformation`.

The `contextSupport` field specifies whether the client supports sending additional information related to the signature help request. If this particular field is supported by the client, it would be ideal to consume the context information to calculate the signature information.

Server Capabilities

Server capabilities are specified with the `SignatureHelpOptions` data model, which contains the following properties.

The `triggerCharacters` field specifies a list of characters where the signature help can be triggered when typed. Depending on the language syntax, the triggers can be varied. In Ballerina language, method call expressions and function call expressions are the scenarios we need to trigger the signature help. According to the syntax, method/function parameters are enclosed within parentheses, and parameters are separated by a comma. Therefore, we can select the `open parenthesis` and the `comma` as the trigger characters for the signature help operation.

The `retriggerCharacters` is a list of characters which will be taken into consideration only when a signature help is active. One of the most common example use cases for this is retriggering the signature help when the user types parameter separator characters (in Ballerina, parameters are separated by commas). Also, all the trigger characters effectively become retrigger characters.

Generating the Signature Help

In our implementation, we use the document URI and the position to capture the symbol at the given position where the signature help is triggered. If the symbol is a valid action invocation, function invocation, or a method invocation, we calculate the signature help for the particular symbol.

As the request parameters, the client sends `SignatureHelpParams` to the server, containing the context property which holds a `SignatureHelpContext` data model. We will be discussing this in detail later in this section.

As a response to the `textDocument/signatureHelp` request, the server sends a `SignatureHelp` data model with the following properties.

The `signatures` property specifies a list of `SignatureInformation` data models which specifies a given signature. The client accepts a list since there are languages which allow overloading function constructs. In our example for the Ballerina language, we only return a single `SignatureInformation` since we do not have an overloading mechanism.

The optional `activeSignature` property specifies the index of the active signature in the signature list. When there are multiple signatures, it is recommended to set this property analyzing the construct for the best possible match.

The optional `activeParameter` property specifies the index of parameters in the parameter list in a `SignatureInformation`. This specifies the currently active parameter, and when we set the property, the client will highlight the particular property and underline them as well as showing the associated documentation.

The `SignatureInformation` contains the following properties.

The `label` property specifies the label to be shown, such as `addNumbers(int number1, int number2)`. When we set the active parameter property for example 0, the client highlights the `number1` part of the label.

The `documentation` property specifies any documentation associated with the function construct. The documentation content can either be a plain string or `MarkupContent` as we discussed in the `textDocument/completion` section.

The `SignatureInformation` model also contains a property called `activeParameter` as we discussed along with the `SignatureHelp` data model. The server can use either of them, but the priority will be given to the `SignatureInformation`'s property when we set both. When it comes to the implementation, the cleaner approach would be to set this property since we can encapsulate all the information associated with a given signature in one place.

The `parameters` property contains a list of `ParameterInformation` data models, which describes the associated information of a parameter in the function, for example, the documentation/description for function parameters which can be extracted from the doc comments of a function.

The `ParameterInformation` also has a few more properties. The `documentation` property specifies the documentation/description associated with the particular parameter.

The label property specifies the parameter label, which can either be a string or a tuple taking two integer values. This information is important for showing the particular parameter highlighted in the label of the signature as we discussed earlier. When the server sets the property with the string value, it should be a substring of the signature label. If we consider our former example, the number1 token is a substring of addNumbers(int number1, int number2). However, we would recommend using the tuple representation to avoid scenarios where substrings appear on the function name as well. The tuple representation specifies a start and end offset range of characters in the label. In our example, for the number1 parameter it will be [11, 23], where the start is inclusive and the end is exclusive.

Listing 6-16. Generating the Signature Help (SignatureProvider.java)

```
public static SignatureHelp
getSignatureHelp(BalSignatureContext context) {
    Optional<FunctionCallExpressionNode> fexpr =
            getFunctionCallExpr(context);
    if (fexpr.isEmpty()) {
        return null;
    }
    int activeParameter = getActiveParameter(context, fexpr.get());
    boolean contextSupport = context.clientCapabilities()
            .getTextDocument().getSignatureHelp()
            .getContextSupport();
    boolean retrigger = context.getParams().getContext().isRetrigger();
    // If retrigger, we return the same
    // signature by changing active parameter
    if (contextSupport && retrigger) {
        SignatureHelp activeSignatureHelp = context.getParams()
                .getContext().getActiveSignatureHelp();
        List<SignatureInformation> signatures =
                activeSignatureHelp.getSignatures();
        for (SignatureInformation signature : signatures) {
            signature.setActiveParameter(activeParameter);
        }
```

```
        return activeSignatureHelp;
    }

    Optional<SignatureInformation> signatureInformation =
            getSignatureInformation(context, fexpr.get(), activeParameter);
    if (signatureInformation.isEmpty()) {
        return null;
    }

    SignatureHelp signatureHelp = new SignatureHelp();
    // Since Ballerina does not have method overriding
    signatureHelp.setActiveSignature(0);
    signatureHelp.setSignatures(Collections
            .singletonList(signatureInformation.get()));

    return signatureHelp;
}
```

Listing 6-16 shows a part of the logic we extracted from the SignatureProvider. java where we evaluate the context information for the signature help request to switch the operational modes of the server. In our example, we check the isRetrigger field to determine whether the signature help is triggered again while a signature help is active in the client. Otherwise, we calculate the signature help by capturing the node information at the given cursor position. When the retriggering occurs, signature help request parameters include the active signature help (activeSignatureHelp) data model. In such cases, the server can reuse the already sent information to save the recomputing cost of certain data. In the example implementation, we check for the trigger character to specify whether the signature help is triggered by the user at the parameter separation token (comma). The client sets the trigger character only if the trigger kind is TriggerCharacter.

This example only shows the starting flow of the implementation. For more details on capturing the documentation, generating parameter labels, and related information, you can refer to the SignatureProvider.java file.

Hover

The textDocument/hover request is sent from the server to the client to request information about a construct when the user hovers the cursor over a token. The hover capability is the quickest way of retrieving information of a construct. In general, the associated information we set for the hover result is extracted from the documentation of a symbol. For example, when we hover over a function call expression, the description and parameter information can be extracted from the doc comments added in the particular function definition. Also, there are scenarios where the server cannot find that information via the doc comments when the user has not added any. In such cases, the server can derive information such as parameter types and return parameters.

Initialization and Capabilities

Client Capabilities

With the HoverClientCapabilities, the client specifies whether it supports the dynamic registration by setting the dynamicRegistration. Also, the client sends a list of MarkupKinds (contentFormat) to specify what MarkupKinds are supported. The order and behavior of the contentFormat are the same as mentioned in the earlier sections. Also, the registration options are specified with the HoverRegistrationOptions data model.

Generating the Hover

The client sends the HoverParams data model as input parameters. The server can extract the document URI and position details enclosed with the TextDocumentPositionParams. In our example use case, we use the document URI to isolate and obtain the semantic model to extract the symbol information at the given cursor position.

As a result for the textDocument/hover request, the server sends a Hover response data model. The server can specify the associated information about the symbol with the contents field set. The contents field can either be a MarkedString, MarkedString[ ], or MarkupContent. As per the protocol specification to date, the MarkedString structure has been deprecated, and therefore we are going to use MarkupContent in our example implementation in HoverProvider.java.

The Hover data structure also contains a range field to specify the associated region of the hover information. This range calculation can be different from one programming language to another based on the syntax and semantic representations, and also the client can interpret the range to highlight the hover range as per the client's desire. Listing 6-17 shows generating the hover result.

Listing 6-17. Generating the Hover Response (HoverProvider.java)

```java
public class HoverProvider {
    ...
    public static Hover getHover(BalHoverContext context) {
        Hover hover = new Hover();
        Path path = context.getPath();
        NonTerminalNode nodeAtCursor = context.getNodeAtCursor();
        Optional<Symbol> symbol = context.compilerManager()
                .getSemanticModel(path).orElseThrow()
                .symbol(nodeAtCursor);

        if (symbol.isEmpty()) {
            return null;
        }
        MarkupContent markupContent = getMarkupContent(symbol.get());
        hover.setContents(Either.forRight(markupContent));

        hover.setRange(toRange(nodeAtCursor.lineRange()));

        return hover;
    }

    private static MarkupContent getMarkupContent(Symbol symbol) {
        Optional<Documentation> documentation;
        MarkupContent markupContent = new MarkupContent();
        StringBuilder content = new StringBuilder();
        markupContent.setKind(MarkupKind.MARKDOWN);
        switch (symbol.kind()) {
            case FUNCTION:
                documentation = ((FunctionSymbol) symbol).documentation();
                break;
```

```java
            case ENUM:
                documentation = ((EnumSymbol) symbol).documentation();
                break;
            default:
                documentation = Optional.empty();
                break;
        }
        documentation.ifPresent(value -> content.append("## Description")
                .append(CommonUtils.MD_LINE_SEPARATOR)
                .append(value.description().orElse(""))
                .append(CommonUtils.MD_LINE_SEPARATOR));

        switch (symbol.kind()) {
            case FUNCTION:
                content.append(((FunctionSymbol) symbol).typeDescriptor().
                signature());
                break;
            case ENUM:
                content.append(((EnumSymbol) symbol).typeDescriptor().
                signature());
                break;
            default:
                break;
        }

        markupContent.setValue(content.toString());

        return markupContent;
    }
    ...
}
```

Summary

In this chapter, we had a look at one of the most commonly used features of language intelligence – the `Diagnostics`. We discussed the representation and how to use the `publishDiagnostics` notification in the Language Server Protocol to send the diagnostics of the source to language clients.

Then we had a look at several request-response pairs in the Language Server to enhance smart editing capabilities. These included `textDocument/completion`, `textDocument/completionItem/resolve`, `textDocument/signatureHelp`, and `textDocument/hover`. All of the aforementioned language features expose a different capability to enhance the developer experience. For features such as auto-completion, the server can utilize the available fields in the `CompletionItem` data structure to achieve and address various aspects related to the developer experience, such as `sortText` and `filterText` for advanced sorting and filtering options and `detail` to provide more information such as documentation associated with a given symbol. Language features such as signature help are used to provide information related to callable units associated with a programming language such as methods and functions. When the user initiates a signature help or the client initiates it by other means, the server can send documentation details for the callable item and its associated parameters. The Hover language feature mainly focuses on providing documentation of a symbol associated with a token in the source. As defined in the programming language, the symbol can be any symbol such as functions, types, classes, enums, etc.

In the next chapter, we are going to look at language features associated with refactorings and code fixes.

CHAPTER 7

Refactoring and Code Fixes

In the previous chapter, we had a look at language features which are used to provide smart editing, documentation support, and diagnostics. When we consider language intelligence, another most useful set of features are refactoring features and code fixes. For example, most of the time the user tends to change variable names, adhere to formatting guidelines, and fix linter issues during the editing process. In this chapter, we are going to look at a set of language features exposed by the Language Server Protocol to achieve refactoring and code fixing capabilities.

Rename

The `textDocument/rename` request is sent from the client to the server to rename a given token/symbol. For example, the user tries to rename a function name/type name. As we are going to look at the next subsection, the `textDocument/prepareRename` can be considered as the prevalidation request for the rename operation. When the user requests a rename over a token, it is the server which has the semantic knowledge to determine whether the particular token can be renamed or not. For example, programming languages have reserved keywords, and the user can mistakenly request a rename for a keyword. In such scenarios, the server can make use of the `prepareRename` support and terminate the operation with a notification. Also, programming languages, such as the Ballerina language, allow the user to use reserved tokens as variable names by escaping them with a single quote (`int 'public = 10; // public is a keyword`). If we consider the last scenario, the user can rename a token to a keyword. Then as a resulting refactor, the server can rename the token to a keyword with a single quote as a prefix. We will be looking at handling this scenario in a more user-friendly manner with the `AnnotatedTextEdits` later in this section.

101

© Nadeeshaan Gunasinghe and Nipuna Marcus 2022
N. Gunasinghe and N. Marcus, *Language Server Protocol and Implementation*,
https://doi.org/10.1007/978-1-4842-7792-8_7

Initialization and Capabilities

Client Capabilities

Client capabilities are specified with RenameClientCapabilities with the following properties.

The dynamicRegistration property specifies whether the client supports dynamic registration of the rename operation.

As mentioned earlier, the rename operation has a supportive operation as prepareRename, and the client specifies whether it supports the prepareRename capability by setting the prepareSupport property.

The prepareSupportDefaultBehaviour specifies the default behavior of the client on selection. The current specification only supports the Identifier selection according to the syntax rules. We will be discussing this in detail later in this section.

The honorsChangeAnnotations specifies whether the rename feature supports change annotations associated with the annotated text edits. For the rename's result, the server can prepare the WorkspaceEdit either with a list of TextEdit models or a list of AnnotatedTextEdits models.

Server Capabilities

Server capabilities are specified with RenameOptions. The server specifies whether it supports the prepareRename operation by setting the prepareProvider property. The client will honor this, only if the client also can support the prepareRename operation.

Listing 7-1 shows how to specify the server capabilities at the initialization of the Language Server.

Listing 7-1. Set Rename Options (ServerInitUtils.java)

```java
public static RenameOptions getRenameOptions() {
    RenameOptions renameOptions = new RenameOptions();
    // Set the prepare support from the server
    renameOptions.setPrepareProvider(true);
    return renameOptions;
}
```

Generating the Workspace Edit

The server responds to the textDocument/rename request with a WorkspaceEdit which applies to the whole workspace. The RenameParams sent with the rename request includes the new name to be used for the renaming which is specified with the newName property. If the new name to be included is valid, then we capture all the references of the particular symbol and generate the workspace edit.

When generating the workspace edit, the server should be aware of the client capabilities such as documentChanges support and changeAnnotationSupport. In Listing 7-2, we use document changes instead of plain changes as well as demonstrate the changeAnnotations. The listing shows how we compute document changes, and for simplicity we have excluded the Ballerina compiler–specific code segments; you can refer to RenameProvider.java for the complete example.

In our example, you can see, when we are looping through the references we found, we check whether our new name is a keyword or not. We mentioned earlier in this section that Ballerina allows the use of keywords as identifiers by escaping them with a single quote. Now, let's say the user is renaming a variable to a keyword:

```
int varName = 123; // user rename varName to int
```

In this scenario, the server can append a single quote to the new name and insert. Although it is not the same value the user expected as the new name, it is a better developer experience to get the user's confirmation before applying the rename changes. We can make use of the AnnotatedTextEdit support to facilitate this requirement. We have defined two ChangeAnnotations as an enum representation for unquoted and quoted edits as shown in Listing 7-3. As shown in Listing 7-2, we use these defined annotations to generate two annotated text edits for a given reference. When the user invokes the rename operation, then the client will show the rename options before automatically applying them, as shown in Figure 7-1. This is one usage of the annotated text edits, and the server can use this capability for use cases such as code actions as well.

> ∨ Quoted Rename Rename keyword with a quote
>   ∨ ■ ☰ core.bal compiler/modules/types
>   ■ int ~~varName~~'int = 123
> ∨ Un-quoted Rename Rename keyword without a quote
>   ∨ ■ ☰ core.bal compiler/modules/types
>   ■ int ~~varName~~int = 123

Figure 7-1. *Annotated text edits for renaming a variable*

If we have a look at our rename document change generation, for the nonkeyword scenarios, we only generate the TextEdits, and the changes will be applied on the source editor without the user's consent.

Listing 7-2. Generate Document Changes for Rename (RenameProvider.java)

```java
private static List<Either<TextDocumentEdit, ResourceOperation>>
getDocumentChanges(BalRenameContext context, String newName) {
    List<Either<TextDocumentEdit, ResourceOperation>>
            textDocumentEdits = new ArrayList<>();
    ...
    Map<String, List<TextEdit>> textEditMap = new HashMap<>();

    for (Module module : modules) {
        ...
        List<Location> references = semanticModel.references(symbol.get());
        // Looping the reference and generate edits
        for (Location reference : references) {
            Range range = toRange(reference.lineRange());
            List<TextEdit> textEdits = new ArrayList<>();
            if (CommonUtils.isKeyword(newName)) {
                /*
                If the new name is a keyword we add annotated edits
                for quoted and unquoted new names
                 */
```

```
                String quotedName = "'" + newName;
                TextEdit quoted = new AnnotatedTextEdit(range,
                        quotedName,
                        RenameChangeAnnotation.withQuote.getId());
                TextEdit plain = new AnnotatedTextEdit(range,
                        newName,
                        RenameChangeAnnotation.withoutQuote.getId());
                textEdits.add(quoted);
                textEdits.add(plain);
            } else {
                textEdits.add(new TextEdit(range, newName));
            }

            String uri = modulePath.resolve(reference.lineRange()
                    .filePath()).toUri().toString();
            if (textEditMap.containsKey(uri)) {
                textEditMap.get(uri).addAll(textEdits);
            } else {
                textEditMap.put(uri, textEdits);
            }
        }
    }
    textEditMap.forEach((uri, annotatedTextEdits) -> {
        TextDocumentEdit textDocumentEdit = new TextDocumentEdit();
        VersionedTextDocumentIdentifier identifier =
                new VersionedTextDocumentIdentifier();
        identifier.setUri(uri);
        List<TextEdit> textEdits = new ArrayList<>(annotatedTextEdits);
        textDocumentEdit.setEdits(textEdits);
        textDocumentEdit.setTextDocument(identifier);
      textDocumentEdits.add(Either.forLeft(textDocumentEdit));
    });

    return textDocumentEdits;
}
```

Listing 7-3. Define Change Annotations for Rename Operation
(RenameProvider.java)

```java
enum RenameChangeAnnotation {
    withQuote("withQuote", "Quoted Rename",
            "Rename keyword with a quote"),
    withoutQuote("withoutQuote", "Un-quoted Rename",
            "Rename keyword without a quote");

    private final String id;
    private final String label;
    private final String description;
    RenameChangeAnnotation(String id, String label, String description) {
        this.id  = id;
        this.label = label;
        this.description = description;
    }

    public ChangeAnnotation get() {
        ChangeAnnotation changeAnnotation = new ChangeAnnotation();
        changeAnnotation.setDescription(this.description);
        changeAnnotation.setLabel(this.label);
        changeAnnotation.setNeedsConfirmation(true);

        return changeAnnotation;
    }

    public String getId() {
        return id;
    }
}
```

Note   At the initialization phase, we capture the workspace capabilities of the
client and then pass down to the language feature APIs accordingly for decision
making. This applies to the particular operation's capabilities as well. For example,
in the rename operation, before sending change annotations, check whether the
client supports the particular capability.

Prepare Rename

The client sends the `textDocument/prepareRename` to the server to validate a renaming operation for a given location. For example, consider the example we discussed in the previous section where the user renames a keyword. As we discussed in the earlier section, both rename and prepare rename are bound together. In the initialization, under the rename capability, the client specifies whether the prepare rename operation is supported.

As the input parameters, the client sends `PrepareRenameParams` containing the position information. The response to the `prepareRename` operation can take the following shapes:

- Range

  The range of the string to be renamed. This is helpful when the user has selected a string with leading and trailing spaces, and then the server specifies the actual range of the token.

- {range: Range, placeholder: string}

  Additional placeholder for the rename input. If the server can generate meaningful names for the variables, this option can be used.

- { defaultBehavior: boolean}

  The rename token identification will be done according to the default behavior of the client.

- Null

  The particular rename operation is not valid at the given location.

In Listing 7-4, we demonstrate the `prepareRename` validation, where the server sends the rename range and a placeholder value as well. This placeholder value is shown in the UI, and the server can either use this placeholder value to provide a hint or a rename's new value suggestion depending on the behavior. Listing 7-5 shows the JSON-RPC format of the `textDocument/prepareRename` response as per our example implementation.

Listing 7-4. Set PrepareRename (RenameProvider.java)

```
public static PrepareRenameResult
    prepareRename(BalPrepareRenameContext context) {
        Token tokenAtCursor = context.getTokenAtCursor();
        if (tokenAtCursor.kind() != SyntaxKind.IDENTIFIER_TOKEN
                || CommonUtils.isKeyword(tokenAtCursor.text())) {
            return null;
        }
        LinePosition startLine = tokenAtCursor.lineRange().startLine();
        LinePosition endLine = tokenAtCursor.lineRange().endLine();
        PrepareRenameResult renameResult = new PrepareRenameResult();
        Range range = new Range();
        range.setStart(new Position(startLine.line(), startLine.offset()));
        range.setEnd(new Position(endLine.line(), endLine.offset()));
        renameResult.setPlaceholder("renamed_" + tokenAtCursor.text());
        renameResult.setRange(range);

        return renameResult;
}
```

Listing 7-5. Prepare Rename JSON-RPC Response

```
[Trace - 8:22:39 AM] Received response 'textDocument/prepareRename - (165)'
in 5ms.
Result: {
    "range": {
        "start": {
            "line": 1,
            "character": 9
        },
        "end": {
            "line": 1,
            "character": 19
        }
    },
    "placeholder": "renamed_helloWorld"
}
```

Formatting

In organizations, you have seen there are specific coding standards being specified. These include best practices such as code organization, naming conventions, and styling guidelines. All these aspects are to ensure the consistency of the code written by the developers in an organization. Among these best practices and coding standards, source code formatting has a significant importance for readability of the code as well as consistency when using version controlling systems. In LSP, the client sends the `textDocument/formatting` request to the server in order to format a document with the specified `TextDocumentIdentifier`. Other than the full document format, the Language Server Protocol allows formatting a section of the document as well, which we will be looking at in the next section.

Initialization and Capabilities

Client Capabilities

Client capabilities are specified with `DocumentFormattingClientCapabilities`, and the client can specify whether it allows the server to dynamically register the formatting operation by setting the `dynamicRegistration` property. In real-world use cases, there are tools/plugins which can be installed to format sources. In such cases, the dynamic registration of the formatting capability is important for Language Server developers. In order to handle such scenarios, we can add user configurations, and based on the configuration values, the server can dynamically register the formatting operation.

Server Capabilities

The server can specify the formatting capabilities via just setting the formatting capability to true or specify with the `DocumentFormattingOptions`. Similarly, the server can register the capability dynamically by setting the `DocumentFormattingRegistrationOptions`.

Generating the Formatting TextEdits

The textDocument/formatting request's input parameters are represented with DocumentFormattingParams. It is important to look at the options property (FormattingOptions) which specifies the options configured and associated with the client. Usually, plugin developers can introduce custom options and read configurations via the configuration operations exposed in the Language Server. Although it is consistent and user-friendly to honor the default editor configuration options, custom configurations can be used to extend the capabilities.

The FormattingOptions exposes the following configurations:

1. tabSize – Size of a tab in spaces

2. insertSpaces – Whether to use tabs or spaces

3. trimTrailingWhitespace – Whether to trim trailing whitespaces of a line

4. insertFinalNewline – Whether to insert a new line at the end of the file

5. trimFinalNewlines – Whether to trim all the new lines at the end of the file

Other than the specified named options, the protocol allows the clients to send more properties as key-value pairs. The type of values can be string, boolean, or number.

In our example (Listing 7-6) use case, we use a formatting library implemented for Ballerina. Currently, the Ballerina formatter library honors a limited number of options.

For the formatting request, the server responds with a list of TextEdits. When generating the TextEdit for the formatting operation, we replace the full document content.

Listing 7-6. Preparing the Formatting (FormatProvider.java)

```java
public static List<TextEdit> format(BaseOperationContext context,
                                    DocumentFormattingParams params) {
    Path path = CommonUtils.uriToPath(params.getTextDocument().
    getUri());
    SyntaxTree syntaxTree = context.compilerManager()
            .getSyntaxTree(path).orElseThrow();
```

```
try {
    // Current ballerina formatter has default behaviour
    // Based on the formatter, formatting options can read and
        utilize
    // FormattingOptions options = params.getOptions();
    String formattedSource = Formatter.format(syntaxTree).
    toSourceCode();
    LinePosition eofPos = syntaxTree.rootNode().lineRange().
    endLine();
    // Replace the full document context
    Range range = new Range(new Position(0, 0),
            new Position(eofPos.line() + 1, eofPos.offset()));
    TextEdit textEdit = new TextEdit(range, formattedSource);

    return Collections.singletonList(textEdit);
} catch (FormatterException e) {
    return Collections.emptyList();
}
}
```

In our example, we do not utilize the formatting options sent by the server, since the current formatter only works on the default options. In cases of using configurable formatters, the server can access the formatting options as `FormattingOptions options = params.getOptions()`. Not only the specified APIs but also the client can send additional properties, which can be accessed as `options.get("propertyName")`. It is always a better practice to use a configurable formatter since the user's default formatting configurations can be honored; otherwise, the server as well as the client can notify the user via logs and documentations on the default behavior of the formatter to avoid conflicts.

Range Formatting

In the previous section, we had a look at the full document formatting for a source, and it is a common requirement in the development flow to format a part/range of a selected text document. This particular capability is exposed in the Language Server Protocol with `textDocument/rangeFormatting`.

Initialization and Capabilities

As we described in the previous section, the client capabilities and server capabilities of the rangeFormatting are similar. In our example, we set the rangeFormatting capability by setting the Boolean flag (instead of using the formatting options) statically upon the initialization request. For the server capability registration at the server initialization, you can refer to BalLanguageServer.java and ServerInitUtils.java, where there are getters for each feature registration option such as getSignatureHelpOptions and getHoverOptions. As a best practice, it is a better option to move all the registration logic to a separate utility/factory implementation to isolate the lengthy logic.

Generating the Range Formatting TextEdits

The textDocument/rangeFormatting request is sent from the client to the server with DocumentRangeFormattingParams. These input parameters include an additional property called range when compared to the DocumentFormattingParams. The options property specified in the parameters is same as we have addressed in the formatting operation earlier. The range specified in the parameters specifies the selection range where the formatting should be applied.

In our example, the Ballerina formatting library allows us to format a range of a text document. In our example implementation in Listing 7-7, we show how to invoke the formatter and to calculate the new range to be included in the TextEdit.

Listing 7-7. Generate the Range Formatting TextEdit (FormatProvider.java)

```
public static List<TextEdit> formatRange(BaseOperationContext context,
                                         DocumentRangeFormattingParams
                                         params) {
    Path path = CommonUtils.uriToPath(params.getTextDocument().
    getUri());
    SyntaxTree syntaxTree = context.compilerManager()
            .getSyntaxTree(path).orElseThrow();
    try {
        // Current ballerina formatter has default behaviour
        // Based on the formatter, formatting options can read and
            utilize
```

```
// FormattingOptions options = params.getOptions();
Range range = params.getRange();
LinePosition startPos = LinePosition.from(
        range.getStart().getLine(),
        range.getStart().getCharacter());
LinePosition endPos = LinePosition.from(
        range.getEnd().getLine(),
        range.getEnd().getCharacter());

LineRange lineRange =LineRange.from(
        syntaxTree.filePath(),
        startPos, endPos);
SyntaxTree formattedTree
        = Formatter.format(syntaxTree, lineRange);

LinePosition eofPos = syntaxTree.rootNode().lineRange().
endLine();
Range updateRange = new Range(new Position(0, 0),
        new Position(eofPos.line() + 1, eofPos.offset()));
TextEdit textEdit = new TextEdit(updateRange,
        formattedTree.toSourceCode());

return Collections.singletonList(textEdit);
} catch (FormatterException e) {
    return Collections.emptyList();
}
}
}
```

Note   For most of the programming languages and scripting languages, there are formatting libraries which address the most common use cases such as tab size, spaces to tab conversion, etc. For the Language Server implementation, we can use such libraries as it is, or the server implementation can use a hybrid approach by modifying the source with external libraries along with the server's specific implementation.

On Type Formatting

The textDocument/onTypeFormatting request is sent from the client to the server to request formatting while typing. The server can configure a set of trigger characters in which the onTypeFormatting should be triggered by the client. We will be looking at the example implementation at the end of this section.

Initialization and Capabilities

Client Capabilities

Client capabilities are specified with DocumentOnTypeFormattingClientCapabilities and include the dynamicRegistration property to specify whether the client supports the dynamic registration of the operation.

Server Capabilities

Server capabilities are specified with DocumentOnTypeFormattingOptions which contains two important properties where the server can specify a set of trigger characters in which the formatting should be triggered.

The firstTriggerCharacter specifies the trigger character for the formatting. Also, the server can specify more trigger characters by setting an array of characters for the moreTriggerCharacter property. In our example use case in Listing 7-8, we are setting "}" as the first trigger character and add ";" to the moreTriggerCharacter list.

Listing 7-8. Set On Type Formatting Options (ServerInitUtils.java)

```
public static DocumentOnTypeFormattingOptions
    getOnTypeFormatOptions() {
    DocumentOnTypeFormattingOptions options = new
    DocumentOnTypeFormattingOptions();
    options.setFirstTriggerCharacter("}");
    options.setMoreTriggerCharacter(Collections.singletonList(";"));
    return options;
}
```

Depending on the language grammar and the semantics of the language, trigger characters can be varied. For example, in most of the language grammars, we have seen the usage of blocks enclosing statements and similar constructs with pairs of braces ("{" and "}"). In such scenarios, typing the closing brace ("}") can indicate completing a valid block, which the server can assume to trigger the formatting for a valid block. In the example use case (Listing 7-8), we have used a semicolon (";") as a trigger character as well. This is because Ballerina's grammar allows the ending of a statement, top-level type definition, and expression with a semicolon, which allows the server to trigger the formatting at the end of a valid construct.

Generating the On Type Formatting TextEdits

The parameters (DocumentOnTypeFormattingParams) of the textDocument/onTypeFormatting contain two main and operation-specific properties as ch and options. The ch property specifies the character typed to trigger the formatting request, and the server can use the trigger character for validations before the formatting. The options property specifies the formatting options which are the same as we discussed in the previous sections.

As a response to the request, the server sends an array of TextEdits to the client. Listing 7-9 shows calculating the formatting TextEdits for the onTypeFormatting. In our example implementation, we have honored on type formatting for function definitions and for local variable declaration only, while the solution can be extended to support a wide range of language constructs according to the semantics. You can use the following example source snippets to test the behavior:

```
function addTwoNumbers      (int number1,      int number2 ) returns int {
        int sum= number1 +      number2;
        // <type } here>

function addTwoNumbers      (int number1,      int number2)          returns
int {
        int sum= number1 +      number2 // <type ; here>
}
```

Note   When you test the feature on VS Code, make sure you enable the **On Type Formatting** option on the user settings.

Listing 7-9. Generate On Type Formatting TextEdit

```
public static List<TextEdit>
onTypeFormat(BalPosBasedContext context,
             DocumentOnTypeFormattingParams params) {
    Path path = CommonUtils
            .uriToPath(params.getTextDocument().getUri());
    SyntaxTree syntaxTree = context.compilerManager()
            .getSyntaxTree(path).orElseThrow();
    try {
        // Current ballerina formatter has default behaviour
        // Based on the formatter, formatting options can read and utilize
        // FormattingOptions options = params.getOptions();
        LineRange lRange;
        NonTerminalNode nodeToFormat = getNodeToFormat(context.
        getNodeAtCursor());
        if ((params.getCh().equals("}")
                && nodeToFormat.kind() == SyntaxKind.FUNCTION_DEFINITION)
                || (params.getCh().equals(";")
                && nodeToFormat.kind() == SyntaxKind.LOCAL_VAR_DECL)) {
            lRange = nodeToFormat.lineRange();
        } else {
            return Collections.emptyList();
        }

        SyntaxTree formattedTree
                = Formatter.format(syntaxTree, lRange);

        LinePosition eofPos = syntaxTree.rootNode().lineRange().endLine();
        Range updateRange = new Range(new Position(0, 0),
                new Position(eofPos.line() + 1, eofPos.offset()));
        TextEdit textEdit = new TextEdit(updateRange,
                formattedTree.toSourceCode());
```

```
        return Collections.singletonList(textEdit);
    } catch (FormatterException e) {
        return Collections.emptyList();
    }
}
```

Note   All three formatting operations we discussed have slightly different behaviors which can be parameterized to work on a common, base implementation. For example, the Ballerina formatting library we used here has a tree visitor which allows formatting a text document or a part of a text document based on the syntax tree. It will take a node into consideration for formatting, and the root node as well as the subtree root is treated in a similar manner.

Code Actions

The client sends the textDocument/codeAction request to the server to compute the commands which can either be code fixes or code refactoring commands. When the server sends the list of CodeActions, the client shows the associated commands in the UI. Then the user can select the particular command, and the client will send a workspace/executeCommand request to execute the actions associated with the particular command.

When we consider a programming language, there are many alternative ways of using the language semantics for achieving the same outcome. Depending on the user's preference, language best practices, organizational guidelines, etc., the choices can vary. Also, it has become a norm today for IDEs and editors to provide error resolving capabilities for the developers by analyzing the semantic and syntactic information of the source. For example, consider the user writes a function name, which is not defined within the scope. In such cases, editors provide quick fixes to generate the particular function within the given scope. The aforementioned use cases are a few of the most widely used refactoring and code fixing options by the developers. The LSP exposes the capability to resolve the aforementioned use cases via code actions.

The server takes the control to specify the supported commands, and those can be registered at the server initialization. In our example use case in Listing 7-10, we have shown registering the commands at the startup.

Listing 7-10. Set Execute Command Options (ServerInitUtils.java)

```
public static ExecuteCommandOptions getExecCommandOptions() {
    ExecuteCommandOptions options = new ExecuteCommandOptions();
    options.setCommands(Arrays.asList(Commands.ADD_DOC,
        Commands.CREATE_VAR));
    return options;
}
```

Initialization and Capabilities

Client Capabilities

Client capabilities are specified with `CodeActionClientCapabilities` which contains the property `dynamicRegistration` to specify whether the client supports registering the operation dynamically.

The protocol allows assigning a kind (`CodeActionKind`) to a code action, and the client can use the kind to group code actions during the presentation in the UI. The `codeActionLiteralSupport` property allows the client to specify the supported set of `CodeActionKind` literals.

The `isPreferredSupport` is an optional property sent by the client to specify whether the client honors setting the `isPreferred` property in a code action. If the client allows setting the particular property, it considers the particular code action for the auto fix command.

The `dataSupport` and `resolveSupport` are associated properties. The client can send a `codeAction/resolve` request to the server in order to retrieve additional information about a certain code action. If the client supports the resolve request, then it should have the data support as well. These data are set by the server as a response to the `codeAction` request, and the same data will be preserved and sent with the `codeAction/resolve` request.

As we had a look at the annotated text edits earlier on the `textDocument/rename` operation, the client specifies whether it supports the annotated text edits for code actions by setting the `honorsChangeAnnotations` property.

Server Capabilities

Server capabilities are specified with the `CodeActionOptions` which contains the following properties.

The `codeActionKinds` property specifies a list of `CodeActionKinds` supported by the server. There are different `CodeActionKinds`, and each is represented with a dot-separated identifier. Here, we will provide a brief description about the available options and example usages:

1. Empty ("")

2. QuickFix ("quickFix")

    For quick fixes which are usually shown when hovering over a diagnostic

3. Refactor ("refactor")

    Code actions such as creating/extracting a variable or a function can be categorized as refactoring code actions

4. Source ("source")

    Code actions in which the effects apply to the whole document such as fix linting issues and organizing imports

5. RefactorExtract ("refactor.extract")

    Such as extracting a variable from a function call which returns a value

6. RefactorInline ("refactor.inline")

    Such as refactoring to an inline function

7. RefactorRewrite ("refactor.rewrite")

    Such as adding an access modifier keyword to a function as a best practice

8. SourceOrganizeImports ("source.organizeImports")

    Code actions which reorganize imports

The first four options are considered as base actions, while the remaining four options are child actions under the base actions. Setting the relevant kind can help in improving the developer experience since the clients in general organize code actions hierarchically with native user experience.

The `resolveProvider` property takes a boolean value to specify whether the server supports the `textDocument/codeAction/resolve` operation.

Generating the CodeAction

Request Parameters

The client sends the `textDocument/codeAction` request with `CodeActionParams` specifying the input data associated with the operation.

The `textDocumentIdentifier` property specifies the text document where the particular code action is triggered.

The `range` property specifies a range where the particular code action is associated with. There are two use cases where the code action is triggered for a given cursor position (both the start and the end of the range are the same), and the code action is triggered for a selection of code blocks (the start and end of the range are different).

The `context` (`CodeActionContext`) property specifies additional information associated with the code action. With the context, the server can access an array of diagnostics (`Diagnostic`) which overlaps with the range of the code action via the `context.diagnostics` property. It is not recommended to use these diagnostics to capture the actual diagnostics for the given range. Depending on the language semantics, diagnostic ranges can be different and should be captured accordingly via semantic APIs or a similar manner. In our example, we simply ignore this particular property and extract the diagnostics by analyzing the range of the text document. Depending on the requirement, the server implementation can use the diagnostics sent with the code action request while it will be a better approach to treat these diagnostics as additional data.

The `only` property in `CodeActionContext` specifies a list of `CodeActionKinds`. If the client sets this particular property, this means the client only considers code actions with the specified code action kind. As we specified earlier, clients can use the code action kind to group the code actions. For example, a client can show only the quick fixes in the context menu using the code action kind as the filter. The servers can honor the `only` property and exclude computing unnecessary code actions by saving the computation time.

Generating the Response

As a response to the `textDocument/codeAction` request, the server sends either an array of Commands or an array of CodeActions. Listing 7-11 is an example for sending commands as the response. Sending just the command is not scalable and informative for the client, since it does not contain additional information as in CodeAction. Once the server sends the command, the client shows the command in the UI, and upon the selection of the certain command, the client sends the `workspace/executeCommand` request to the server. Then the server can proceed with the workspace edit operations for the particular command.

Listing 7-11. Generate a Command as a Response (CodeActionProvider.java)

```java
public static List<Either<Command, CodeAction>>
getCodeAction(BalCodeActionContext context, CodeActionParams params) {
    List<Either<Command, CodeAction>> codeActions = new ArrayList<>();
    List<Diagnostic> diags = getDiagnostics(context, params.getRange());
    Optional<Node> topLevelNode =
        getTopLevelNode(context, params.getRange());
    List<String> diagMessages = diags.stream()
        .map(diag -> diag.message().toLowerCase(Locale.ROOT))
        .collect(Collectors.toList());
    if (diagMessages.contains(VAR_ASSIGNMENT_REQUIRED)) {
      Diagnostic diagnostic = diags.get(diagMessages
          .indexOf(VAR_ASSIGNMENT_REQUIRED));
      Command createVarCommand =
          getCreateVarCommand(context, diagnostic,
              params.getRange());
      Either<Command, CodeAction> command =
          Either.forLeft(createVarCommand);
      return Collections.singletonList(command);
    }
    ...
}
```

```
private static CommandgetCreateVarCommand(BalCodeActionContext context,
        Diagnostic diagnostic,
        Range range) {
    String expr = context.getNodeAtCursor().toSourceCode().trim();
    Command command = new Command();
    command.setCommand(BalCommand.CREATE_VAR.getCommand());
    command.setTitle(BalCommand.CREATE_VAR.getTitle());
    List<Object> args = new ArrayList<>();
    String typeDescriptor = getExpectedTypeDescriptor(range, context);
    String uri = context.getPath().toUri().toString();
    String newText = typeDescriptor + " varName = " + expr;
    LineRange lineRange = context.getNodeAtCursor().lineRange();
    CreateVariableArgs createVarArgs =
        new CreateVariableArgs(newText, lineRange, uri, diagnostic);
    args.add(new CommandArgument("params", createVarArgs));
    command.setArguments(args);
    return command;
}
```

When sending CodeActions as the response, the server can set the kind of the code action. The Language Server Protocol specifies levels of code action kinds. Depending on the requirement, the server can either set a generic kind such as CodeActionKind. Refactor or a more fine-grained kind such as RefactorExtract. If both the client and the server can support code action literals, it would be better to set the code action kind meaningfully to provide a rich developer experience. The example in Listing 7-12 demonstrates the usage of CodeActionKind.QuickFix (the CodeAction variation of Listing 7-11), and Figure 7-2 shows how the client (VS Code) presents quick fixes for the developer in the user interface.

```
1    function addTwoNumbers(int a, int b) returns int {
2        return a + b;
3    }
4         variable assignment is required (BCE2526)
5    publ  View Problem (⌥F8)   Quick Fix... (⌘.)
6    💡   addTwoNumbers(10, 20);
7    }
```

Figure 7-2. *VS Code's representation of quick fixes for diagnostics*

Listing 7-12. Generate a CodeAction

```
private static CodeAction
    getCreateVarCodeAction(BalCodeActionContext context,
                            Range range,
Diagnostic diagnostic,
CodeActionParams params) {
    CodeAction codeAction = new CodeAction();
    codeAction.setTitle(Command.CREATE_VAR.getTitle());
    codeAction.setKind(CodeActionKind.QuickFix);
    /*
    Setting the diagnostic will show a quickfix link when hover over the
    diagnostic.
    */
    codeAction.setDiagnostics(Collections
            .singletonList(getDiagnostic(diagnostic)));
    codeAction.setEdit(getWorkspaceEdit(context, range));
    ...
    return codeAction;
}
```

The diagnostics field takes a list of diagnostics that the particular code action resolves. If the particular code action is generated for a given diagnostic, then the client can use the particular diagnostics to provide various visual aids such as shown in Figure 7-2.

The `isPreferred` property can be set for a code action if the server expects that particular action is appropriate to be executed with the auto fix command. It is a more common behavior that there are multiple code actions for a given construct/diagnostic. In our example in Listing 7-12 where we have shown that we generate a code action for creating a variable, when we set the `isPreferred` property, the client will automatically apply the code action upon the auto fix command execution. When setting the field for a particular code action, the server should ensure that the particular code action addresses the resolution provided properly. Otherwise, the output of the code action might not address user expectations, and the user will have to spend cycles to revert certain unexpected changes.

The `disabled` property can be set by the server to disable a certain code action. Then the client should honor the following guidelines specified as in the protocol.

Disabling code actions for certain contexts completely depends on the language semantics and the implementation of the Language Server. For example, let's consider a code action which extracts a set of statements to a function. In certain scenarios, compilers could not be able to compute the correct type information during the type checker phase if there are syntax errors which cannot be recovered in a predictable manner. One such situation is when there are multiple syntax errors. In such situations, the code action might not be able to properly capture the type information which is required to generate a new function encapsulating the statements. In these scenarios, the server can set the disabled property for the code action with an appropriate error message.

The `edit` property takes a `WorkspaceEdit` to be applied upon the selection of the code action. Calculating the workspace edit for a code action can take a while in certain scenarios. For example, consider a code action which generates an undefined function where the server has to extract the types of the arguments, the return types, as well as the location of the source. In such cases, the code action can skip setting the workspace edit and use the resolve request to compute the particular workspace edit on demand. The `CreateFunctionCodeAction.java` is an example that we will be discussing in the next section.

The `command` property allows the server to set a command associated with the code action. One important thing which should be kept in mind is, if the server sets both the `edit` property and the `command` property for the code action, the client will apply the workspace edit first, and then trigger the command. Also, when the server implementation does not support the resolve operation, still the server can avoid computing the edit for time-consuming scenarios and achieve the same via setting the `command` property and handling the workspace edit upon the `workspace/executeCommand` request.

The data property can be set by the server to preserve any data between codeAction and resolve requests. Usually, these data can be some metadata to decide the appropriate context information, without recalculating them as in the codeAction request. The context information captured in the codeAction request can be populated in the data property and reused in the resolve request. We will be looking at an example in the next section of this chapter.

Code Actions Resolve

The codeAction/resolve request is sent from the client to the server for requesting additional information for a code action. As described in the previous section, the client specifies whether it supports the code action resolve operation with the client's code action capabilities. The client specifies the support by setting the resolveSupport with a list of properties where the client allows it to resolve with the resolve request. Listing 7-13 is a part of a trace message extracted for the code action request which specifies the supported properties to be resolved.

Listing 7-13. CodeAction Client Capabilities

```
"codeAction": {
    "dynamicRegistration": true,
    "isPreferredSupport": true,
    "disabledSupport": true,
    "dataSupport": true,
    "resolveSupport": {
        "properties": [
            "edit"
        ]
    },
    "codeActionLiteralSupport": {
        "codeActionKind": {
            "valueSet": [
                "",
```

```
            "quickfix",
            "refactor",
            ...
        ]
    }
},
"honorsChangeAnnotations": false
}
```

The `CreateFunctionCodeAction.java` demonstrates generating a code actions to create a function and we fill the `data` property with the location information which will be preserved for reference in the `codeAction/resolve` request. The input parameter of the request is a `CodeAction`, and the result/response is also a `CodeAction` with the resolved parameters filled. The `CreateFunctionCodeActionResolve.java` shows generating the edit for the response code action.

CodeLens

The `textDocument/codeLens` request is sent from the client to the server to request code lenses for the document. Code lens shows a clickable hovering link on the document which executes a command upon selection when available.

Initialization and Capabilities

Client Capabilities

Client capabilities (`CodeLensClientCapabilities`) of the codelens specify whether it allows dynamic registration of the operation with the `dynamicRegistration` property.

Server Capabilities

Server capabilities (`CodeLensOptions`) allow the server to specify whether it supports the code lens resolve support. This approach is slightly different from the code action and code action resolve request as we discussed in the previous section. When the server sets the `resolveProvider` property, then the client sends the `codeLens/resolve` to the server, to get the command to be executed upon the selection of the code lens.

Generating the Response

The client sends the CodeLensParams for the server which includes the document identifier for the document where the code lens request is triggered. The code lens request is not triggered for the cursor positions, instead for the full document. When the text document is modified, then the client sends a codeLens request again to recompute the code lenses.

As a response to the textDocument/codeLens request, the server sends an array of CodeLenses.

The range property in the CodeLens specifies the range where the particular code lens is associated with. It is important that the range should cover a single line.

The command property specifies the command to be executed upon the selection of the particular code lens. This is an optional property to set during the textDocument/codeLens operation. If the server needs to perform a heavy computation to define the command, then the server can get the benefit of the resolve request to calculate the command upon request. The next section looks at an example for the resolve request.

The data field is the same as the data field we discussed in the textDocument/codeAction request. The data field is preserved during the textDocument/codeLens and the codeLens/resolve request, and the server can fill metadata which is required to capture and compute the command for the code lens at the resolve request. The example in Listing 7-14 shows computing the code lens for adding documentation for a public function. In cases where the server needs to carry out heavy computation to compute the command for the CodeLens, then the server can set required metadata to the data field and depend on the resolve request to compute the relevant command.

Listing 7-14. CodeLens for Documenting a Public Function

```
public static List<CodeLens>
getCodeLenses(BalCodeLensContext context, CodeLensParams params) {
    List<FunctionDefinitionNode> functions = getPublicFunctions(context);
    List<CodeLens> codeLensList = new ArrayList<>();
    for (FunctionDefinitionNode function : functions) {
        CodeLens codeLens = new CodeLens();
        org.eclipse.lsp4j.Command command = new org.eclipse.lsp4j.
        Command();
        command.setCommand(BalCommand.ADD_DOC.getCommand());
```

```
        command.setTitle(BalCommand.ADD_DOC.getTitle());
        List<Object> args = new ArrayList<>();
        String fName = function.functionName().text();
        String uri = context.getPath().toUri().toString();
        args.add(new CommandArgument("params", new AddDocsArgs(fName,
        uri)));
        command.setArguments(args);
        codeLens.setCommand(command);
        // The range is set to the function name.
        // It is a must, that the range spans for a single line
        codeLens.setRange(toRange(function.functionName().lineRange()));
        codeLensList.add(codeLens);
    }

    return codeLensList;
}
```

CodeLens Resolve

The client sends the codeLens/resolve request to the server to resolve an associated command for the code lens. As described in the previous section, if the server supports the resolve request, then the server can avoid setting the command in the CodeLens response sent to the client, and the client can send the resolve request to request the code lens with the command.

The client sends the resolve request with CodeLens as an input, and this will preserve the data property's content set at the codeLens response. These data filled in the data property can be used as metadata during the resolve as described in the previous section.

CodeLens Refresh

The server sends the workspace/codeLens/refresh request to the client to refresh/recalculate all the code lenses in the workspace. According to the Language Server Protocol, it is strongly recommended to use this request in special cases such as configuration changes which can affect the project and can cause recomputation of the code lenses. The client specifies whether it can support the refresh request by setting the refreshSupport property in CodeLensWorkspaceClientCapabilities. In our example implementation, we register a file watch for the Ballerina.toml configuration file, and, upon the workspace/didChangeWatchedFiles notification, the server sends the refresh request to the client. The BalWorkspaceService.java contains the didChangeWatchedFiles method where we have addressed this scenario; registering the file watch will be described in a later chapter in detail.

Summary

When it comes to composing the source codes in IDEs/text editors, the developers frequently carry out various refactorings such as formatting and symbol renaming. Also, IDEs and editors provide code fixes by analyzing the sources and based on the enforced best practices and linting rules.

The Language Server Protocol provides the renaming capability to allow renaming language constructs. Depending on the implementation, the server can define whether to rename only the symbols or extend the capability to support other workspace constructs such as keywords and so on.

In the protocol, there are three types of formatting options provided as formatting a given document, formatting a range of a given document, and formatting while typing. These capabilities can leverage the developer experience when used in an effective manner. Specially, the onTypeFormatting capability should not be used excessively with a bunch of trigger characters. Depending on the language semantics, the server can limit the trigger points leading to an effective developer experience.

Most of the time, language smartness providers suggest code refactorings, enforcing language best practices, for example, optimizing loop constructs. With the Language Server Protocol, the server can provide such capabilities with code actions. Code actions can be used not only to refactor a single document but also to refactor the entire workspace.

In this chapter, we discussed the refactoring features exposed by the Language Server Protocol. When it comes to the developer experience, navigation through the code is also very important. In the next chapter, we are going to discuss about code navigation features exposed by the Language Server Protocol.

CHAPTER 8

Code Navigation and Navigation Helpers

When composing a code, nine out of ten times the users refer to already defined information. For example, consider a use case of searching all the usages of a function. Code navigation features such as references, definitions, and declarations are used frequently to navigate between semantic references of language constructs. In this chapter, our focus is to have an understanding of the code navigation features supported by the Language Server Protocol.

Reference

The `textDocument/references` request is sent from the server to the client to get all the references of a symbol. For a given source file, compilers generate symbols including semantic information. When we consider a function definition as an example, there are numerous usages in the same document as well as in other documents depending on the source structuring. If the programming language allows to structure the source documents within packages/modules, then the references of the function symbol in a given project can be scattered in more than one document among multiple packages/modules in the project. In more advanced use cases, you have seen that IDEs navigate to the references in external dependencies as well. As an example, IntelliJ IDEA allows you to find references of the constructs of sources coming from Maven modules. In each of these use cases, the server implementation should ensure to honor the semantic meaning of a symbol within the given project, and this information is captured via the compiler APIs provided by the particular compiler. In our example

131

© Nadeeshaan Gunasinghe and Nipuna Marcus 2022
N. Gunasinghe and N. Marcus, *Language Server Protocol and Implementation*,
https://doi.org/10.1007/978-1-4842-7792-8_8

use case for the Ballerina language, a Ballerina project[1] can be a single document or a set of documents organized into modules. In such a scenario, a symbol reference can be used in different documents in the same module or in other modules as well. The reference implementation can scale to the magnitude depending on the capabilities of the compiler to capture symbol references in the whole project, and the concept of the project can vary depending on the programming language.

When we consider programming languages, the developers use libraries provided by third parties. If we consider the usage of a construct from a third-party library (public function), the developers would be interested to find the references of the particular symbol as well. Therefore, if we consider the references in a project we should consider the symbols defined within the same project as well as in other projects/libraries.

The implementation can be extended to more advanced use cases such as in scenarios where there are multiple projects opened in a single workspace and then finding the references in other projects in the same workspace as well.

Client Capabilities

Client capabilities are specified with the ReferenceClientCapabilities which includes the dynamicRegistration property to specify whether the client allows to dynamically register the capability.

Server Capabilities

Server capabilities can be specified with the ReferenceOptions, or the server can use the boolean flag to register the capability. You can refer to ServerInitUtils.java to observe the capability initiation for each of the operations.

Generating the Response

The request parameters for the references request (ReferenceParams) contain the context property which has the ReferencesContext. The references context specifies one property – includeDeclaration – which specifies whether the client expects the server to include the declaration of the particular reference as well. If the particular

---

[1]https://ballerina.io/learn/user-guide/ballerina-packages/creating-your-first-ballerina-package/

property is set, then the server should include the location of the particular symbol's declaration as well. Consider the example Ballerina code in Listing 8-1 where we consider the variable message. If the client has set the includeDeclaration property, we include the location of the variable declaration in line 2, which includes two resulting location entries in the response when the user requests the reference of the message variable in line 3.

Listing 8-1. Ballerina Code to Print a Message

```
import ballerina/io;
function helloWorld(string name) {
    string message = "Hello " + name + "!";
    io:println(message);
}
```

As a response to the request, the server sends back an array of Locations. A location includes the URI of the document where the particular reference resides as well as the range of the reference's identifier (e.g., the start and end of the variable name). The example in Listing 8-2 shows finding the references of the symbols in a Ballerina source as well as generating the response. The references API provided in the Ballerina compiler's semantic API accepts a flag to consider capturing the declaration of a reference as well. Hence, as we described earlier, we use the includeDeclaration property in the ReferencesContext as the input to the API. You can refer to ReferencesProvider.java for more information on using Ballerina's compiler APIs to find the references of a symbol.

Listing 8-2. Generating the References (ReferencesProvider.java)

```
public static List<Location> references(BalReferencesContext context) {
        List<Location> locations = new ArrayList<>();
        boolean includeDeclaration =
                context.getReferenceContext().isIncludeDeclaration();
        // Capture the references from Ballerina Compiler APIs
        Map<Module, List<io.ballerina.tools.diagnostics.Location>> references
                = findReferences(context, includeDeclaration);
```

```
    // Generate the references response
    references
            .forEach((module, locationList) -> locationList
                    .forEach(location ->
                            locations.add(toLspLocation(module,
                            location)))));

    return locations;
}
```

Definition

The textDocument/definition request is sent from the client to request the definition information of a symbol. As we described in the previous section, the developer experience expands to many use cases such as referring to the definition of a symbol originated from an external library. The definition of a symbol/language construct is important in many scenarios during the development. It is true that documenting a publicly exposed language construct gives an understanding of the behavior of language constructs. For example, consider adding documentation for a Ballerina function. As we discussed in Chapter 6, we can show quick information about the language construct when hovering over the function call expression, or we can show the information during auto-completions by setting the description. Now, if we consider private constructs within the same project, the developers frequently refer to the existing implementation to observe the behavior. In such scenarios, quickly navigating to the definition is a must-have capability. The textDocument/definition provides this capability to quickly navigate the definition of a particular language construct/symbol.

Client Capabilities

Client capabilities are specified with DefinitionClientCapabilities which includes two properties as dynamicRegistration and linkSupport. The dynamicRegistration property is the same as we discussed earlier. The client can set the linkSupport property to specify whether the server can send additional information with a documentation link. We will be looking at the documentation link later in this section.

Server Capabilities

Server capabilities are specified with `DefinitionOptions` or with the `boolean` flag. You can refer to `ServerInitUtils.java` for generating the capabilities.

Generating the Response

The `textDocument/definition` request parameters are defined as `DefinitionParams`. The client specifies the location of the referencing symbol with the text document's URI and the cursor position.

The response for the definition request can be one of the four options:

1. Location

2. Location[]

3. LocationLink[]

4. Null

We will be looking into these options next in this section.

A `Location` as a response can be considered when there is only one definition for the given symbol. In our example scenario for Ballerina, we have shown in Listing 8-3 how to generate the definition response for a Ballerina symbol.

Listing 8-3. Definition for Ballerina – a List of Locations (DefinitionProvider.java)

```
public static List<Location>
definition(BalDefinitionContext context) {
    // Ballerina semantic API facilitate an API to find the symbol and from
       that we get the definition
    ...
    Optional<Symbol> symbol =
            semanticModel.symbol(document, linePos);
    if (symbol.isEmpty()) {
        return Collections.emptyList();
    }
```

```
io.ballerina.tools.diagnostics.Location location =
        symbol.get().getLocation().orElseThrow();

return Collections.singletonList(toLspLocation(location));
}
```

In Ballerina, you can have methods defined in a class as we have shown in Listing 8-4. Also, a class can have an object as a type reference. In such scenarios, the methods declared in the object can be defined within the class. If a user invokes the definition request for a method call expression – as the getName() usage within the main function – we can send both locations as an array of Locations.

Listing 8-4. Class Definition in Ballerina

```
type Person object {
    function getName() returns string;
    function getAge() returns int;
};

class Student {
    *Person;
    private string name;
    private int age;
    private string school;
    function init(string name, int age, string school) {
        self.name = name;
        self.age = age;
        self.school = school;
    }
    function getSchool() returns string {
        return self.school;
    }
    function getName() returns string {
        return self.name;
    }
    function getAge() returns int {
        self.age;
    }
}
```

```
public function main() {
    Student student = new("Bob Alex", 16, "Mt. View College");
    string name = student.getName();
}
```

The implementation is similar to Listing 8-3, while only the symbol capturing logic is different. Let's consider a programming language such as Java, which allows method/function overloading. When providing the definition support for partially completed sources – such as method calls with empty arguments leading to semantic errors – the servers can provide all the possible definitions of the overloaded methods with the same name/identifier semantics. In this scenario, the list of Locations as the response is the ideal solution.

Instead of the Locations, the server can send a list of LocationLinks as the response to the definition request. The LocationLink is a richer data model than the Location, since it allows the server to set the following fields with the addressed capabilities.

The originSelectionRange specifies the range of the symbol which is used as the invoking symbol of the definition request. This is an optional property, and in this case, the client will tokenize the words and select the word at the cursor.

The targetUri is the document URI where the actual definition resides.

The targetRange specifies the full range which encloses the symbol. If the symbol is a variable definition such as int message = "Hello World";, then the targetRange will be from the start (character i) to the end (semicolon) of the variable.

The targetSelectionRange is the range of the message symbol identifier in the definition. In our variable definition example, this would be the range of the message token which is inside the targetRange. It is important to make sure that the targetSelectionRange should be enclosed by targetRange. The DefinitionProvider.java demonstrates the LocationLink generation in detail.

In order to provide a better user experience, it is always a good choice to use the LocationLink list as the response. The server should make sure that the client also supports the LocationLink which is set in the client capabilities via the linkSupport.

Listing 8-5 shows the usage of LocationLink as the response to the textDocument/definition request.

Listing 8-5. LocationLink as the Response to the Go-to Definition
(DefinitionProvider.java)

```
public static List<LocationLink>
definitionWithLocationLink(BalDefinitionContext context) {
    // In this implementation we only consider the definition
    // of the constructs in the same project.
    ...
    Optional<Symbol> symbol =
            semanticModel.symbol(document, linePos);
    if (symbol.isEmpty()) {
        return Collections.emptyList();
    }
    io.ballerina.tools.diagnostics.Location location
            = symbol.get().getLocation().orElseThrow();

    LocationLink locationLink = new LocationLink();
    NonTerminalNode nodeAtCursor = context.getNodeAtCursor();
    Range originRange = toRange(nodeAtCursor.lineRange());
    Range targetRange = toRange(location.lineRange());
    locationLink.setOriginSelectionRange(originRange);
    locationLink.setTargetRange(targetRange);
    locationLink.setTargetSelectionRange(targetRange);
    locationLink.setTargetUri(getUri(context, symbol.get(), location));

    return Collections.singletonList(locationLink);
}
```

Type Definition

The textDocument/typeDefinition request is sent from the client to request the type
definition location of a symbol. For example, consider the example Ballerina source in
Listing 8-6.

Listing 8-6. Ballerina Code with Record Type Definition

```
import ballerina/io;
public function main() {
```

```
    Person bob = {
        name: "Bob",
        age: 30
    };
    io:println(bob.name);
};
public type Person record {
    string name;
    int age;
};
```

The Person record at the top level is a type definition in Ballerina. In our main function, we have created a variable bob, and next we access the field name. If we consider the bob.name expression and execute the type definition against bob, then the server navigates the user to the Person type definition.

The observation for the type definition comes in handy when the developers face issues such as type mismatch errors in statements and expressions. One of the most common usage is when using method call/function call expressions, and the provided arguments (say already defined variables) are having different/mismatched types. Without going back and forth to the definition of a variable to find the actual type, the use of the type definition feature makes life easier.

Client Capabilities

Client capabilities are specified with DefinitionClientCapabilities which includes two properties as dynamicRegistration and linkSupport. The dynamicRegistration property is the same as we discussed earlier. The client can set the linkSupport property to specify whether the server can send additional information with a documentation link. The usage of the linkSupport is the same as we discussed in the "Definition" section.

Server Capabilities

Server capabilities are specified with TypeDefinitionOptions or with the boolean flag, while registration options are specified with TypeDefinitionRegistrationOptions. You can refer to ServerInitUtils.java for generating the server capabilities.

Generating the Response

The response for the typeDefinition request can be one of the four options as we described in the definition request:

1. Location

2. Location[]

3. LocationLink[]

4. Null

Listing 8-7 shows generating the response for the typeDefinition request. All the concepts we discussed in the "Definition" section regarding response variations can be applied as it is for the typeDefinition response as well.

Listing 8-7. Calculating the Type Definition (DefinitionProvider.java)

```java
public static List<Location>
    typeDefinition(BalTypeDefContext context) {
        ...
        Optional<Symbol> symbol =
                semanticModel.symbol(document, linePos);
        if (symbol.isEmpty()) {
            return Collections.emptyList();
        }
        /*
        Capture the type symbol of the given symbol
         */
        TypeSymbol typeSymbol =
                CommonUtils.getTypeDefinition(symbol.get()).orElseThrow();
        io.ballerina.tools.diagnostics.Location location =
                typeSymbol.getLocation().orElseThrow();

        return Collections.singletonList(toLspLocation(location));
}
```

Implementation

The textDocument/implementation request is sent from the client to the server to request the implementation of the symbol at the cursor position. The implementation request is generally valid for function calls/method calls. If we consider a programming language such as Java, the implementation of an interface also can be linked with this request. The example in Listing 8-8 shows an object type descriptor Animal and two class definitions (Cat and Dog) referencing the Animal type definition. In our example, when the user requests the implementation of the talk method, the server responds to the client with the location of the Cat or Dog's talk methods.

Listing 8-8. Ballerina Code for the Implementation Request Example

```
type Animal object {
    public function talk();
};
class Cat {
    *Animal;
    public function talk() {
        io:println("Meow!");
    }
}
class Dog {
    *Animal;
    public function talk() {
        io:println("Woof!");
    }
}
public function main() {
    Cat cat = new();
    cat.talk();
}
```

Client Capabilities

Client capabilities are specified with `ImplementationClientCapabilities` which includes two properties as `dynamicRegistration` and `linkSupport`. The `dynamicRegistration` property is the same as we discussed earlier. The client can set the `linkSupport` property to specify whether the server can send additional information with a documentation link. The usage of the `linkSupport` is the same as we discussed in the "Definition" section.

Server Capabilities

Server capabilities are specified with `ImplementationOptions` or with the `boolean` flag, while registration options are specified with `ImplementationRegistrationOptions`. You can refer to `ServerInitUtils.java` for generating the server capabilities.

Generating the Response

The response for the `implementation` request can be one of the four options as we described in the definition request:

1. Location

2. Location[]

3. LocationLink[]

4. Null

Listing 8-9 shows generating the response for the `implementation` request. All the concepts we discussed in the "Definition" section regarding response variations can be applied as it is for the `implementation` response as well.

Listing 8-9. Ballerina Code for the Implementation Request Example (DefinitionProvider.java)

```
public static List<Location>
implementation(BalGotoImplContext context) {
    ...
    Position cursorPos = context.getCursorPosition();
```

```
LinePosition linePos = LinePosition.from(cursorPos.getLine(),
        cursorPos.getCharacter());
Optional<Symbol> symbol =
        semanticModel.symbol(document, linePos);
/*
Implementation is only allowed for method symbols.
*/
if (symbol.isEmpty()
        || symbol.get().kind() != SymbolKind.METHOD) {
    return Collections.emptyList();
}
io.ballerina.tools.diagnostics.Location location =
        symbol.get().getLocation().orElseThrow();

return Collections.singletonList(toLspLocation(location));
}
```

Declaration

The textDocument/declaration request is sent from the client to request the declaration of a symbol in a given position.

Client Capabilities

Client capabilities are specified with DeclarationClientCapabilities which includes two properties as dynamicRegistration and linkSupport. The dynamicRegistration property is the same as we discussed earlier. The client can set the linkSupport property to specify whether the server can send additional information with a documentation link. The usage of the linkSupport is the same as we discussed in the "Definition" section.

Server Capabilities

Server capabilities are specified with DeclarationOptions or with the boolean flag, while registration options are specified with DeclarationRegistrationOptions. You can refer to ServerInitUtils.java for generating the server capabilities.

Generating the Response

The response for the `declaration` request can be one of the four options as we described in the definition request:

1.   Location

2.   Location[]

3.   LocationLink[]

4.   Null

Listings 8-3 and 8-9 showed generating the responses for the `definition` and `implementation` requests. When we look at the implementations, one common behavior we can identify is that symbol capturing and location data model generation is similar, while the particular symbol (definition/implementation of the symbol) identification logic is different, and, similarly, the response generation of the `declaration` takes the same approach.

Document Symbol

The `textDocument/documentSymbol` request is sent from the client to the server requesting symbols in a text document. The server is supposed to send all the symbols in the document regardless of the scoping and the visibility. For example, a particular document can have symbols with the same identifier literal residing in different scopes. The list of document symbols can be organized as a flat list of symbols or a hierarchical list of symbols. We will be discussing these approaches at the end of this section.

Client Capabilities

Client capabilities are specified with `DocumentSymbolClientCapabilities`.

The `dynamicRegistration` property specifies whether the client allows the server to register the `documentSymbol` capability dynamically after the initialize request.

The `symbolKind` property specifies the set of symbol kinds supported by the client, and when this particular property is set, the client guarantees to gracefully handle the unknown symbol kinds sent by the server. If the property is not set, the protocol specification specifies that only the symbol kinds defined from `File` to `Array` will be supported (as per the initial protocol specification). The symbol kind allows the developers to get a quick glance at the symbol list and distinguish them. For example, the server responds to the documentSymbol request with all the symbols regardless of the scoping. Then there can be different symbols in different scopes with different types depending on the symbol scoping defined in the language. In such scenarios, the symbols can be distinguished by setting the SymbolKind for the symbol. In general, the clients use different icons to distinguish the symbols based on the SymbolKind set for the symbol. The hierarchicalDocumentSymbolSupport specifies whether the client can support/handle symbol hierarchy representation. We will be discussing this later in this section.

The tagSupport specifies whether the client can support symbol tags. If the client sets this property, it should send the supported list of tags. Currently, the Language Server Protocol specifies a single tag that is the Deprecated tag. When the server sets the Deprecated tag for a symbol, the user interface, in general, will render the particular item with a strikethrough. In the earlier versions of the protocol before introducing the tag support, the deprecated property in DocumentSymbol was supposed to be used in order to specify that the symbol has been obsolete. Since the particular property has been deprecated in the latest protocol, the server is supposed to use the tags.

The label property allows the server to set a label for the particular symbol resolver.

Server Capabilities

Server capabilities for the documentSymbol are represented with DocumentSymbolOptions. When initializing the server capabilities, the server can set the label for the provider by setting the label property. It is better to set the property since the client can use the name to differentiate the document outlines when there are several for the same document. Editors such as VS Code allow the extension developer to write their own code outlines with the extension rather than the default outline. If you carefully observe the trace logs once you open a document in the editor, there is a trace entry for the documentSymbol operation even without the user's execution of the particular command. This is for populating the outline of the opened text document.

Generating the Response

The DocumentSymbolParams specifies the input parameters for the documentSymbol operation which includes the text document identifier.

As a response to the documentSymbol request, the server can respond with one of the following:

1. SymbolInformation[]

2. DocumentSymbol[]

3. Null

Using SymbolInformation

The name, kind, and location are mandatory properties for the SymbolInformation. The kind will be used by the client to render the symbol in a distinguishable manner such as assigning a unique icon to the symbols with a particular kind. The location property specifies the range where the particular symbol resides in the given text document. Depending on the language construct, the server can decide which should be the location range. For example, the server can either set the symbol identifier's range (start and end of the identifier) or the whole construct. If we consider the int total = a + b; statement, when we set the range of the variable total as the whole statement's range, it can do no harm to the presentation. If we set the range for a function definition in this manner, then it might not make sense. Therefore, depending on the language semantics, the server can decide which range to be selected. In our example use cases, we will be using the identifier location for consistency.

The containerName can be set to specify a name for a symbol enclosing the current symbol. This is not a scalable usage to organize the symbols in the parent-child hierarchy. If the server wishes to expose this hierarchy, it is strongly recommended to use the DocumentSymbol instead.

Listing 8-10 shows how the symbol information as a response is generated, and Figure 8-1 shows how VS Code visualizes the symbols in the user interface. This example only captures the definition and function parameters of Ballerina, and the same concept can be extended to support the complete language grammar. Depending on the language implementation and semantics, symbol grouping and symbol capturing can be varied.

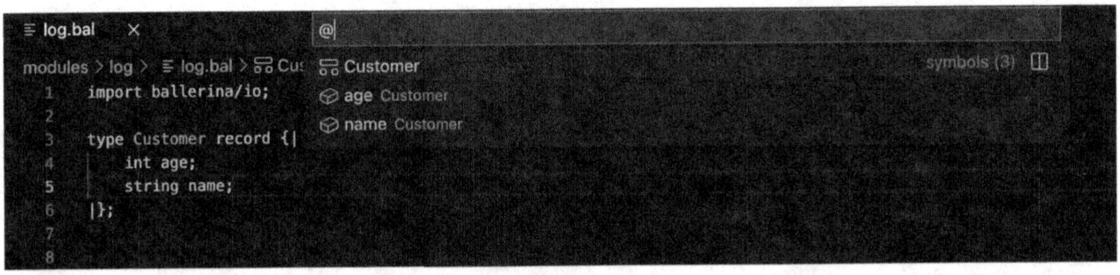

Figure 8-1. *VS Code showing the document symbols for SymbolInformation*

Listing 8-10. Generate Symbol Information (DocumentSymbolProvider.java)

```java
public static List<Either<SymbolInformation, DocumentSymbol>>
getSymbolInformation(BalDocumentSymbolContext context) {
    ...
    for (ModuleMemberDeclarationNode member : members) {
        SymbolInformation funcInfo = new SymbolInformation();
        if (member.kind() == SyntaxKind.FUNCTION_DEFINITION) {
            FunctionDefinitionNode functionDef =
                    (FunctionDefinitionNode) member;
            ...
            funcInfo.setKind(SymbolKind.Function);
            funcInfo.setName(((functionDef).functionName().text());
            ...
            if (isDeprecatedFunction(context, functionDef)) {
                funcInfo.setTags(Collections.singletonList
                (SymbolTag.Deprecated));
            }
            // Generate the symbols for the function parameters
            SeparatedNodeList<ParameterNode> parameters =
                    functionDef.functionSignature().parameters();
            for (ParameterNode parameter : parameters) {
                String paramName;
                SymbolInformation paramInfo = new SymbolInformation();
                ...
                paramInfo.setKind(SymbolKind.TypeParameter);
                paramInfo.setName(paramName);
                ...
```

```
            /*
            Add the parameter under the function symbol
            to represent the hierarchy
             */
            paramInfo.setContainerName(funcInfo.getName());
            symbols.add(Either.forLeft(paramInfo));
        }
        symbols.add(Either.forLeft(funcInfo));
      }
   }
   return symbols;
}
```

Using DocumentSymbol

The name, kind, and tags fields are the same as we discussed in the SymbolInformation subsection. The DocumentSymbol allows to set a detail property to specify additional information for the symbol. The server can set metadata such as the resolved type, return type of a function symbol, signature of a type/function symbol, documentation, etc., in this field. In our example, we are going to use the type of a variable symbol and the return type of a function symbol to fill the detail field.

The range and selectionRange fields are two important fields in a DocumentSymbol. The range field specifies a range enclosing the particular symbol. As the protocol specifies, this range should be defined excluding the leading and trailing whitespaces. For example, if we consider module-level constructs in Ballerina such as type definitions and functions, we consider the range including access modifiers and the construct's body. If we consider a variable definition, the range would be including access modifiers. Then the selectionRange specifies the range to be selected when the client navigates to the particular symbol. We can set the identifier of the particular symbol, and it is required that the selectionRange is enclosed by the range.

As we discussed in the previous subsection, the SymbolInformation allows setting a containerName to enclose a symbol with a top-level symbol, which is not consistent and scalable for complex scenarios. Therefore, the DocumentSymbol allows setting the children of a certain symbol via the children property. In our use case, we are going to set the fields of a record symbol as the children of the particular record type definition.

Listing 8-11 shows generating the DocumentSymbols as the response.

Listing 8-11. Generate the Document Symbol (DocumentSymbolProvider.java)

```
public static List<Either<SymbolInformation, DocumentSymbol>>
getDocumentSymbol(BalDocumentSymbolContext context) {
    ...
    for (ModuleMemberDeclarationNode member : members) {
        ...
        DocumentSymbol recordSymbol = new DocumentSymbol();
        TypeDefinitionNode typeDef =
                (TypeDefinitionNode) member;
        ...
        recordSymbol.setKind(SymbolKind.Struct);
        // Set the range and selection range
        ...
        recordSymbol.setRange(range);
        recordSymbol.setSelectionRange(selectionRange);
        // Generate the symbols for the record fields
        NodeList<Node> fields = ((RecordTypeDescriptorNode)
                typeDef.typeDescriptor()).fields();
        List<DocumentSymbol> children = new ArrayList<>();

        for (Node field : fields) {
            Token fieldName;
            DocumentSymbol fieldSymbol = new DocumentSymbol();
            ...
            fieldSymbol.setKind(SymbolKind.Field);
            fieldSymbol.setName(fieldName.text());
            ...
            // Add the field as a child
            children.add(fieldSymbol);
        }
        recordSymbol.setChildren(children);
        if (CommonUtils.isDeprecated(member)) {
            recordSymbol.setTags(Collections
                    .singletonList(SymbolTag.Deprecated));
        }
```

```
        symbols.add(Either.forRight(recordSymbol));
    }
    return symbols;
}
```

Document Highlight

As we discussed at the beginning of this chapter, it is an important requirement for the developers to find the references of a given symbol. One of the drawbacks of the usage of the references request to find the references of a given symbol is that the user has to execute the specified key combination or use the context menu to find the references. The reason for mentioning this behavior as a drawback is when we consider the requirement of locating the references of a symbol in the current document or around the cursor. This requirement is important to get a quick glance at the usages instead of the big picture, and as a result, the response of the highlighting request is allowed to be more fuzzy than the references request. Also, the solution for this requirement should minimize context switching as in finding the references. As a solution, the textDocument/documentHighlight request is sent from the client to the server for requesting the symbol references to be highlighted. The client specifies the symbol to be extracted with positional parameters (document URI and cursor position), and the client highlights the references of the particular symbol. In general, the request is initialized by the client when the user positions the caret on a symbol.

Client Capabilities

Client capabilities are specified with DocumentHighlightClientCapabilities which includes the dynamicRegistration property which specifies whether the client supports dynamically registering a capability.

Server Capabilities

Server capabilities are specified with DocumentHighlightOptions or with the boolean flag, while registration options are specified with DocumentHighlightRegistrationOptions. You can refer to ServerInitUtils.java for generating the server capabilities.

Generating the Response

The client sends the DocumentHighlightParams containing the positional information for the symbol references to be extracted.

The server generates an array of DocumentHighlight constructs as a response to the request. The range property of the DocumentHighlight specifies the range of the text document to be highlighted for the particular reference. Usually, this range is the identifier range of the particular reference. One of the important properties of this construct is the kind (DocumentHighlightKind). There are three kinds defined in the current protocol specification as follows:

1. Text

2. Read

3. Write

Let's consider the source snippet in Listing 8-12 and the variable message. For the variable, we have one place where we assign the value and one place where we read the variable value. In order to distinguish the usage, the server can set the kind analyzing the semantic information of the symbol. Listing 8-13 shows generating the document highlight response with the kind information derived with the semantic information. When the client presents the different kinds of highlights to the users, usually they use different background colors to highlight the particular ranges.

Listing 8-12. Ballerina Source with Variable Read and Write

```
public function main() {
    string message = getMessage();
    io:println(message);
}
function getMessage() returns string {
    return "Hello World";
}
```

Listing 8-13. Generating Document Highlight (DocumentHighlightProvider.java)

```java
public static List<DocumentHighlight>
getHighlight(BalDocumentHighlightContext context) {
    SemanticModel semanticModel = context.compilerManager()
            .getSemanticModel(context.getPath()).orElseThrow();
    Document document = context.compilerManager()
            .getDocument(context.getPath()).orElseThrow();
    Position position = context.getCursorPosition();
    LinePosition linePos = LinePosition.from(position.getLine(),
            position.getCharacter());
    List<Location> references =
            semanticModel.references(document, linePos);

    List<DocumentHighlight> highlights = new ArrayList<>();

    for (Location location : references) {
        LinePosition sLine = location.lineRange().startLine();
        LinePosition eLine = location.lineRange().endLine();
        Position start = new Position(sLine.line(), sLine.offset());
        Position end = new Position(eLine.line(), eLine.offset());
        Range range = new Range(start, end);

        DocumentHighlight highlight = new DocumentHighlight();
        highlight.setRange(range);
        if (isWrite(context, location)) {
            highlight.setKind(DocumentHighlightKind.Write);
        } else {
            highlight.setKind(DocumentHighlightKind.Read);
        }
        highlights.add(highlight);
    }

    return highlights;
}
```

Document Link

The client sends the `textDocument/documentLink` request to the server to resolve the links in a text document identified by the text document identifier. In scenarios such as file access and external endpoint access, the developers include the document URIs or web URIs in a source code. With the document link capability, the server can specify the ranges in the text documents where the document or web resource links can be found. This feature is important in most cases where the users can quickly navigate the particular resource and check whether the resource is available for access during the development time. In Ballerina, HTTP client endpoints accept a URI.

Client Capabilities

The `DocumentLinkClientCapabilities` specifies the `dynamicRegistration` which is the same as we discussed in earlier sections as well. The other important property in the capabilities is the `toolTipSupport`, which specifies whether the client accepts a tooltip associated with the given document link. We will be having a look at the importance and usage in our examples shown later in this section.

Server Capabilities

The `DocumentLinkOptions` holds the important property `resolveProvider` which specifies that the server can support the `documentLinkResolve` request. We will be looking at the usage and functioning of the resolve request in the next section.

Generating the Response

The client sends the `DocumentLinkParams` specifying the `textDocument(TextDocumentId entifier)` for the document to calculate the links.

As a response, the server sends an array of `DocumentLink` data structures to the client including the following properties.

The `range` specifies the text range in the document where a particular link appears.

The `target` specifies the resource link appearing in the given range of the document. This field is optional, and if the server does not set the particular field, the client will send a resolve request to get the target, and the server should set the corresponding capability at the server initiation.

Depending on the language constructs and the APIs, there can be scenarios where the particular link cannot be extracted just using a regular expression or any other pattern matching methods. Additional processing such as accessing the semantic constructs and getting the required data to resolve a target URL can take time. The server can avoid such additional information processing during the documentLink request and calculate the actual accessible URL on the resolve request. If the server needs to preserve metadata to be captured during the resolve request, those can be set in the data property.

The data property which is an optional property is also associated with the resolve request where the information set in the particular property will be preserved with the documentLink and documentLinkResolve requests.

The toolTip property specifies information associated with the particular link. These can be instructions to access/navigate the link or description about the particular URL. If the server can extract them, it is a better option to set the tooltip since the developer can have an initial glance at the link when hovering over the range. This can even avoid the user visiting the link to get information about the link which saves time and avoids the developer's context switching.

Listing 8-14 shows generating the DocumentLinks for a document.

Listing 8-14. Generating the Document Link (DocumentLinkProvider.java)

```
public static List<DocumentLink>
getDocumentLink(BalDocumentLinkContext context) {
    Map<LineRange, String> linkRanges = getLinkRanges(context);
    List<DocumentLink> documentLinks = new ArrayList<>();
    /*
    Here we set the target. Target can also be
    calculated from the resolve request
     */
    linkRanges.forEach((lineRange, target) -> {
        DocumentLink link = new DocumentLink();
        if (context.clientCapabilities().getTextDocument()
                .getDocumentLink().getTooltipSupport()) {
            link.setTooltip("cmd/ ctrl + click to navigate");
        }
        Range range = toRange(lineRange);
        link.setRange(range);
```

```
    /*
    Preserve the document URI in the data field.
    This will be referred during the resolve request
    */
    // Map<String, String> dataMap = new HashMap<>();
    // dataMap.put(DOC_URI,
    // context.params().getTextDocument().getUri());
    // link.setData(dataMap);
    link.setTarget(target);
    documentLinks.add(link);
    });

    return documentLinks;
}
```

Document Link Resolve

The client sends the documentLink/resolve request to the server to resolve the target of a DocumentLink. As described in the earlier section, the server can initiate the resolve operation support with the document link capabilities. The resolve support is important when the target of the link has to be calculated with additional meta information such as values assigned to the variables.

The input parameters of the resolve operation are a DocumentLink, and the data property set in the documentLink response will be preserved here. In our example in Listing 8-14, we preserve the document URI in the data field to refer to during the resolve request.

Listing 8-15 shows resolving the target of a DocumentLink.

Listing 8-15. Generating the Document Link for the Resolve Request

```
public static DocumentLink
getDocumentLinkResolved(BaseOperationContext context, DocumentLink documentLink)
{
    /*
    Extract the document Uri from data field
    */
```

```
    String uri = ((JsonObject) documentLink.getData()).get(DOC_URI).
    getAsString();
    Path path = CommonUtils.uriToPath(uri);
    String target = getTarget(context, path, documentLink.getRange());
    DocumentLink link = new DocumentLink();
    link.setTooltip(documentLink.getTooltip());
    link.setRange(documentLink.getRange());
    link.setTooltip(documentLink.getTooltip());
    link.setTarget(target);
    return link;
}
```

Summary

When using the editors and IDEs by the developers, it is a common requirement to navigate to the existing programming constructs. For example, the developers use features such as jumping to the definition and finding the symbol references frequently. In this chapter, we had a look at navigation features such as definition and references as well as navigation helper features such as the document symbol, document highlight, and document link.

All these features are used by the developers with different weights as per their preferences. In this chapter, we had a look at the various capabilities provided by each of these features and how to utilize them to provide a better developer experience, and now you are in a position to explore more features related to the selection of constructs such as individual tokens, code blocks, as well as features which focus on the representation of the language semantics. In the next chapter, we are going to look at presentation and selection features in detail.

CHAPTER 9

Presentation and Selection

Consider an IDE and features such as showing color palettes/color pickers. When it comes to conventional coding, such features can be considered as enhancement features. In the previous chapters, we had a look at language features which guide the developers while providing suggestions, finding references, as well as allowing the developers to carry out refactoring operations based on both semantic and syntactic knowledge. Even though all these features are essential for a smartness provider, the user experience can be further enhanced and made smooth with the help of enhancement capabilities which we are going to discuss in this chapter. In this chapter, we are going to look at a feature category which is basically enhancement features focusing on the presentation of information and selection capabilities. Among them, semantic highlighting of tokens, color representations with palettes, folding language constructs, call hierarchy, and token/construct selection such as selection range will be discussed in detail.

Semantic Tokens

Text editors and IDEs provide syntax highlighting to improve the meaning of language semantics. Different IDEs and text editors use contrasting techniques for highlighting sources by tokenizing. For example, in order to provide a syntax highlighter[1] for a new language in VS Code, the extension developer can create a TextMate grammar for the particular language. For the IntelliJ IDEA, the concept is different and uses TextAttributeKeys[2] to highlight the tokens.

---

[1] https://code.visualstudio.com/api/language-extensions/syntax-highlight-guide
[2] https://plugins.jetbrains.com/docs/intellij/syntax-highlighting-and-error-highlighting.html

157

© Nadeeshaan Gunasinghe and Nipuna Marcus 2022
N. Gunasinghe and N. Marcus, *Language Server Protocol and Implementation*,
https://doi.org/10.1007/978-1-4842-7792-8_9

Likewise, each plugin has to use a different syntax highlighting implementation for each language. When we consider a programming language, what the user sees on the editor's UI is not only the text but also the semantic meaning of the constructs. Therefore, when it comes to syntax highlighting, the user naturally expects the semantic meaning to be represented on the token highlighting as well. If you consider both approaches for highlighting we mentioned earlier, those are in general token-based highlighting. In a programming language's point of view, this is the syntactic information. The compilers have a parsing phase (lexical and syntactic analysis) which considers the syntactic meaning of the source, and after this phase, the compilers go through the semantic analyzing phase to enrich the abstract syntax tree (AST) with semantic information. This semantic phase provides different meanings for the tokens based on scoping and various other grammar rules in the language's specification. For example, the semantic analyzing phase can distinguish between a local variable declaration and a function parameter. Now, when we consider syntax highlighting, such complex information cannot be represented by just analyzing the syntax itself. If you consider the TextMate grammar, it is nearly impossible to achieve such behavior.

In order to avoid this, the Language Server Protocol has defined the semantic token feature. Semantic token support should not be used to completely replace client-specific syntax highlighting, and the intention is to enhance the highlighting capability with semantic information. This is because, when it comes to highlighting the tokens based on the semantic information, grammar-based approaches cannot achieve the desired expectations as we discussed earlier, for example, highlighting all the variable references with the same color in all the places.

The client sends the semantic token requests to the server requesting semantic tokens in a document. The semantic token request has four variations as follows, and we will be discussing each of them in this section:

1. textDocument/semanticTokens/full

2. textDocument/semanticTokens/full/delta

3. textDocument/semanticTokens/range

4. workspace/semanticTokens/refresh

Client Capabilities

Client capabilities are specified with `SemanticTokensClientCapabilities` where the following properties are available.

The `dynamicRegistration` field specifies whether the client supports the dynamic registration of the semantic token operation.

The `requests` field is a hierarchical field specifying the support of request variations 1–3, which we mentioned earlier. The `requests.range` field specifies whether the client supports the `textDocument/semanticTokens/range` request. If the `request.full` field is a boolean, the client specifies it only supports the `textDocument/semanticTokens/full` request. If the client wants to specify the support for `textDocument/semanticTokens/full/delta`, the client can set the `requests.full.delta` field.

The `tokenTypes` specifies the supported list of tokens by the client. These token types will be used to highlight the tokens semantically.

The `tokenModifiers` field specifies the supported list of token modifiers by the client. The server can use token modifiers along with the token type to distinguish the semantic tokens. When highlighting the tokens, the client uses both the token type and the token modifier to define the color of the tokens.

The `tokenFormat` specifies the list of token formats supported by the protocol. Currently, the protocol supports only the `relative` token format which specifies that the tokens are represented with relative positions.

The `overlappingTokenSupport` specifies that the client supports the tokens which are overlapping.

The `multilineTokenSupport` specifies whether the client supports highlighting the tokens spread in multiple lines. In general, a single token cannot spread in multiple lines. However, when it comes to cases such as semantically highlighting tokens such as regular expression strings, which can spread to more than one line, the multiline token support is beneficial.

Server Capabilities

Server capabilities are specified with the `SemanticTokensOptions` which includes the following properties, and registration options are specified with `SemanticTokensRegistrationOptions`.

The legend field specifies a legend of semantic token types and token modifiers which will be used for integer encoding and decoding of the tokens. The server sends a SemanticTokensLegend to the clients which includes the tokenTypes property, which is a list of token types supported by the server, and the tokenModifiers property, which is a list of token modifiers supported by the server. When encoding and decoding token type integers, both the server and the client use the indexes of the lists.

The range field specifies whether the server supports the textDocument/semanticTokens/range request. It is always recommended to the server for supporting the semantic token feature for ranges, since the clients use this for highlighting the minimap.

The full property specifies whether the server supports the textDocument/semanticTokens/full request. Also, the server can specify the textDocument/semanticTokens/full/delta support by setting the full.delta property.

Generating the Response

Semantic Tokens for Whole Document – full

The client sends the SemanticTokensParams as the request parameters which includes the TextDocumentIdentifier.

As a response, the server sends either a SemanticTokens data model or null. The SemanticTokens data model contains the resultId property which specifies a string identifier which will be used by the clients when sending subsequent semantic token delta requests. The data property specifies the actual list of tokens to be highlighted. The actual token is represented via an encoded unsigned integer.

Semantic Tokens for Whole Document – full/delta

The client sends the SemanticTokensDeltaParams as the request parameters which includes the TextDocumentIdentifier and the previousResultId pointing to the resultId generated for the last semantic token request or the semantic token delta request.

Note   During the implementation of the delta request, the server has to maintain the status in order to correlate the subsequent request IDs.

As a response, the server can either send SemanticTokens or SemanticTokensDelta data models. In an error scenario, a null is also accepted. The SemanticTokensDelta model contains an optional resultId which will be sent to the server by the client in subsequent delta requests. Also, the edits property sends the list of SemanticTokensEdit which is used to transform the previous result to new semantic tokens. The corresponding previous result is identified by the resultId associated with the delta request as mentioned earlier.

The SemanticTokensEdit model contains three properties: start, the start offset of the edit; deleteCount, the number of tokens to be deleted; and data, a list of tokens to be inserted. All of these are calculated as relative information to a referencing start token.

Responding with a SemanticTokensEdit model is not always possible given the type of edit done in the source. For example, if the user enters a new line in the source, the server can easily calculate the token edit. If the user removes a block of code including a function declaration, the server has to recalculate the semantic model and perform the token identification. Depending on the compiler's behavior and the type of edit, the server can decide which approach is better. If the server wishes to use the benefit of both approaches, that is also possible as per the protocol.

Semantic Tokens for a Range – range

The client sends the textDocument/semanticTokens/range request to get the semantic tokens for a given range. One of the most frequent uses of the range request is to get the semantic tokens to highlight the minimap. The protocol recommends implementing the range request at the server, if the client supports the range request. If the clients use a minimap, then minimap highlighting also can be consistent with the source, and it will provide a smooth developer experience.

Listing 9-1 shows calculating the semantic tokens for the semanticTokens/full request. In the example implementation, the reader can refer to the SemanticTokensProvider.java class for the implementation of other variations as well as the detailed implementation of features. The getSemanticTokensInRange method handles calculating the semantic tokens for a range. In our implementation, the logic is the same as in the getSemanticTokens method, and we do an additional range check for language constructs.

If we have a look at the static field SEMANTIC_TOKENS_LEGEND, this is the legend we are using when we register the capability. In ServerInitUtils.java we set the server capabilities as we described in the earlier chapter.

Our implementation has been limited for type definitions for demonstration purposes, and the solution can be extended to support other language constructs as well by using the semantic APIs available.

Listing 9-1. Implement semanticTokens/full for Type Definitions (SemanticTokensProvider.java)

```
public static SemanticTokens
getSemanticTokens(BalSemanticTokenContext context) {
    SyntaxTree syntaxTree = context.currentSyntaxTree().get();
    List<Integer> data = new ArrayList<>();
    Map<Integer, Token> lastTokenInLine = new HashMap<>();
    int lastLine = 0;
    ModulePartNode modPart = syntaxTree.rootNode();
    for (ModuleMemberDeclarationNode member : (modPart).members()) {
        // filter only the type definitions
        if (member.kind() != SyntaxKind.TYPE_DEFINITION) {
            continue;
        }
        Token typeName =
        ((TypeDefinitionNode) member).typeName();
        LinePosition startLine =
        typeName.lineRange().startLine();
        int startChar = startLine.offset();
        if (lastTokenInLine.containsKey(startLine.line())) {
            // captures the token offset relative
            // to last token of a given line
            startChar = startChar - lastTokenInLine
                    .get(startLine.line()).lineRange()
                    .startLine().offset();
        }
        int line = startLine.line() - lastLine;
        lastLine = startLine.line();
        lastTokenInLine.put(line, typeName);
        int length = typeName.text().length();
        int tokenType =
```

```
        TOKEN_TYPES.indexOf(SemanticTokenTypes.Type);
        int tokenModifiers =
                (1 << MODIFIERS.indexOf(SemanticTokenModifiers.
                Declaration))
                | (1 << MODIFIERS.indexOf(SemanticTokenModifiers.
                Definition));
        data.add(line);
        data.add(startChar);
        data.add(length);
        data.add(tokenType);
        data.add(tokenModifiers);
    }

    return new SemanticTokens(data);
}
```

Encoding and Decoding a Token

Earlier, we mentioned that the tokens are being encoded by the server and decoded by the client to extract the token information for highlighting. The main reason for using an encoding scheme is because the number of semantic tokens in a given document can be a large number. The data field of response models holds a list of unsigned integers which represent a token. A given token is represented by five subsequent integers. Consider the following index representation[3] where i is a positive integer starting from 0:

- (5*i) – Token line relative to the previous token.

- (5*i + 1) – Start character of the token. If two tokens are in the same line, then the values are calculated relative to the first token. Otherwise, they are relative to zero.

- (5*i + 2) – Token length.

- (5*i + 3) – Token type as per SemanticTokensLegend.

---

[3] https://microsoft.github.io/language-server-protocol/specifications/
specification-3-16/#textDocument_semanticTokens

- (5*i + 4) – Token modifiers. When defining the value, consider the zero-based index of each of the token modifiers which is going to assign and set each bit of the binary sequence and then convert to a decimal. Refer to **Table 9-1**.

Let's consider an example scenario explaining the aforementioned set of values. Figure 9-1 shows us two lines with column numbers where we have defined two variables.

	1	2	3	4	5	6	7	8	9	10	11	12	13	14	15	16	17	18	19	20	21	22
1	i	n	t		a	g	e		=			3	2	;								
2																						
3	s	t	r	i	n	g		n	a	m	e			=		"	B	o	b	"	;	
4																						

Figure 9-1. *Line and column numbers of variables*

Now consider the following two lists for the semantic token legend and token modifiers:

1. Semantic token legend

   ['namespace', 'type', 'variable', 'parameter']

2. Token modifiers

   ['declaration', 'readonly', 'static', 'deprecated']

Now, let's define the index values for tokens int, age, and name. Since we have three tokens, we have 15 entries in the token list. Also, for the representation, consider the variable age is a deprecated variable.

Table 9-1. *Semantically Encoded Token Values*

Token Name	(5*i)	(5*i) + 1	(5*i) + 2	(5*i) + 3	(5*i) + 4
int	1	1	3	('type') = 1	0b000000 = 0 (no modifiers)
age	(1 - 1) = 0	(5 - 1) = 4	3	('variable') = 2	0b001001 = 9 ('declaration', 'deprecated')
name	3	8	4	('variable') = 2	0b000001 = 1 ('declaration')

Document Color

The client sends the `textDocument/documentColor` to the server, requesting the color information in a text document. If we consider an example use case such as in CSS, it is a common scenario where the developers specify color information. In such cases, you have observed that there are colored boxes and popped up color palettes on editing. The Language Server Protocol allows to facilitate such features via the `documentColor` operation. This particular operation is not a common feature to be used with all languages; instead, the server's implementation varies depending on the programming language semantics.

Client Capabilities

Client capabilities are specified with `DocumentColorClientCapabilities` where the client specifies whether it supports dynamic registration by setting the optional `dynamicRegistration` property.

Server Capabilities

The server can set the capability by setting the `boolean` flag, setting the `DocumentColorOptions` if it wants to use the progress capabilities, or setting the `DocumentColorRegistrationOptions`.

Generating the Response

The client sends the `DocumentColorParams` which includes the `textDocument` property to get the document information.

As a response, the server sends an array of `ColorInformation`. A given `ColorInformation` specifies a `range` property and `color` property. The range property specifies the text range where the particular information is associated with. The `color` property specifies a color data model that has red, green, blue, and alpha fields which accept a decimal value (0–1). In other words, the color data model describes a color in the RGBA format.

Since in the Ballerina language there are no first-class semantics which utilize colors, for demonstration purposes, we are going to use an annotation which can be added to a function parameter to specify that the particular parameter specifies a color value. Then, we will generate the color information for the arguments. Consider Listing 9-2 which shows the example Ballerina source for the described use case.

165

Listing 9-2. Ballerina Source with the Color Annotation

```
annotation Colour on parameter;
function printColour(@Colour string colour1, @Colour string colour2) {
    ...
}
public function main() {
    printColour("255, 111, 12, 1", "200, 111, 12, 1");
}
```

Listing 9-3 shows generating the color response, and Figure 9-2 shows how the color information is represented in VS Code for our use case.

Listing 9-3. Generating the Response for documentColor (DocumentColourProvider.java)

```
public static List<ColorInformation>
getColours(BalDocumentColourContext context) {
    ...
    for (FunctionDefinitionNode function : functions) {
        ...
        // Iterate over parameters
        for (int i = 0; i < parameters.size(); i++) {
            ParameterNode param = parameters.get(i);
            ...
            // Comes to this point, only if the
            // function has the colour annotation

            // get all the references of function
        // and capture the colour values
            List<Location> references = semanticModel.references(symbol.
            get(), false);
            // Convert RGB string to
            Map<Range, List<Double>> rgbInfo = getRGB(references, i,
            context, path);
            rgbInfo.forEach((range, floats) -> {
                Color color = new Color(floats.get(0),
                        floats.get(1),
```

```
                    floats.get(2),
                    floats.get(3));
            ColorInformation colorInformation = new
            ColorInformation(range, color);
            colorInformations.add(colorInformation);
        });
      }
    }
    return colorInformations;
}
```

```
annotation Colour on parameter;
Add Documentation
function printColour(@Colour string colour1, @Colour string colour2) {

}
Add Documentation
public function main() {
    printColour( ■"255, 111, 12, 1", ■"200, 111, 12, 1");
}
```

Figure 9-2. Color information shown before the RGBA value string

Color Presentation

In the previous section, we looked at how to send the color information for a given text document. Now let's consider a scenario where the client shows a color palette, and the user selects one of the colors. Then the client needs to insert the particular color value in the source. If we consider the documentColor operation, the server identifies the color information depending on the language semantics. For example, the source might contain the color information in Hex format even though the protocol accepts the RGB format. Therefore, when the user selects a color from the palette, the new color should be converted to a value which is acceptable by the language semantics.

In order to support this particular use case, the client sends the textDocument/colorPresentation request to get the associated text edits for the picked color.

167

There are no separate registration options for the operation, and instead it behaves as a resolve request for the documentColor. By registering the documentColor support, the server specifies the colorPresentation support as well.

Generating the Response

The client sends a ColorPresentationParams data model as the input parameters. The data model includes the textDocument property specifying the text document associated with the request. The color property specifies the color information (RGBA) value for which the server should generate the presentation. In other words, we can consider the color property represents the new color selected by the user from the color palette. The range property specifies where the color value would be inserted.

As a response, the server sends a list of ColorPresentation data models to the client. The presentation value specifies the text ranges to be changed with the newly selected color value which is sent with the colorPresentation request. The ColorPresentation contains the following properties.

The label property specifies a text label for the particular color representation. This label is shown as the header of the color picker.

The textEdit property specifies the text edit which should be applied upon the selection of the color value. This property is an optional field, and in case of absence, the label will be used.

The additionalTextEdits property specifies the additional edits which need to be added on the selection of the color value. It is important to keep in mind that the additional text edits should not overlap the main text edit's range.

Listing 9-4 shows generating the response for the colorPresentation, and Figure 9-3 depicts how VS Code shows the information on the user interface.

Listing 9-4. Generating the Response for colorPresentation (DocumentColourProvider.java)

```java
public static List<ColorPresentation> getColourPresentation(
        ColorPresentationParams params) {
    TextEdit textEdit = new TextEdit();
    Color color = params.getColor();
    textEdit.setRange(params.getRange());
    String insertColour = "\"" + Math.round(color.getRed() * 255) + ", " +
```

```
                Math.round(color.getGreen()) * 255 + ", " +
                Math.round(color.getBlue()) * 255 + ", " +
                Math.round(color.getAlpha()) + "\"";
        textEdit.setNewText(insertColour);
        ColorPresentation presentation = new ColorPresentation();
        presentation.setLabel(insertColour);
        presentation.setTextEdit(textEdit);

        return Collections.singletonList(presentation);
    }
}
```

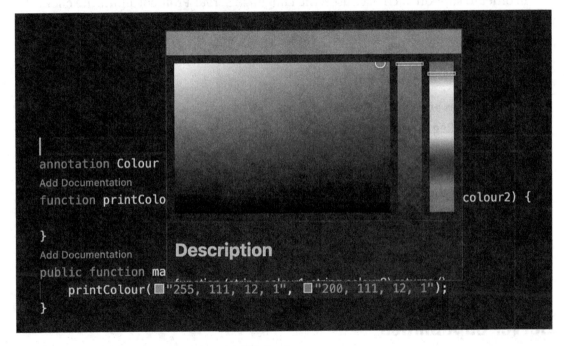

Figure 9-3. *Color presentation in VS Code*

Folding Range

The clients usually detect code blocks to fold based on character pairs such as open and close braces. However, there are certain scenarios where the language semantics only can infer the folding of the blocks, such as imports and comments. In certain programming languages such as Python, there are no open and close brace pairs for language constructs such as a for loop as shown in Listing 9-5. Even though there is no marked boundary with character pairs, it should be possible to handle such scenarios. In most of the cases, modern IDEs and text editors have the built-in capability to identify the blocks by character pairs such as braces, while special language constructs as in Listing 9-5 need to be handled specifically.

Listing 9-5. Python For Loop

```
countries = ["Sri Lanka", "China", "Australia"]
for x in countries:
  print(x)
```

In order to support such use cases, the Language Server Protocol allows the clients to send the textDocument/foldingRange request to get folding ranges from the server.

Client Capabilities

Client capabilities are specified with FoldingRangeClientCapabilities.

The dynamicRegistration field specifies whether the client allows dynamically registering the capability.

The rangeLimit specifies the number of folding ranges accepted by the client. It is not necessary for the server to acknowledge the limit value specified by the client. In such cases, the client will drop the excess range values.

The lineFoldingOnly field specifies whether the client supports only the line-based folding. In such cases, even if the server has set the start character and the end character, the client will ignore them.

Server Capabilities

The server can set the capability by setting the boolean flag, setting the FoldingRangeOptions if it wants to use the progress capabilities, or setting the FoldingRangeRegistrationOptions.

Generating the Response

The client sends FoldingRangeParams with the request. The input parameter data model includes the textDocument field specifying the text document for which the folding ranges are requested.

As a response, the server sends a list of FoldingRange data models. A given FoldingRange includes the following fields.

The startLine specifies the starting line of the folding range, and the startCharacter specifies the starting character of the folding range. Similarly, the fields endLine and endCharacter specify the ending line and the ending column of the folding range. All these line and character values are considered as zero-based values.

The kind field specifies the kind of the folding range. Earlier in this section, we specified that there can be various constructs which can fold. In editors, there are commands/key bindings to fold a collection of constructs such as comments. The current protocol defines three kinds as Comment, Imports, and Region. Listing 9-6 shows generating the response for the foldingRange request (the extracted snippet only shows generating the folding range for imports).

1. Comment – Specifies that the range contains comments. The server can use this kind to both subsequent single-line comments and block comments.

2. Imports – Specifies that the range contains imports.

3. Region – Any other constructs such as function bodies, looping constructs' bodies, etc.

Listing 9-6. Generating the Response for foldingRange (FoldingRangeProvider.java)

```java
public static List<FoldingRange> getFoldingRanges(
        BalFoldingRangeContext context) {
    NodeList<ImportDeclarationNode> imports = modulePartNode.imports();
    if (!imports.isEmpty() && imports.size() > 1) {
        ImportDeclarationNode firstImport = imports.get(0);
        ImportDeclarationNode lastImport = imports.get(imports.size() - 1);

        LinePosition strtLine = firstImport.lineRange().startLine();
        LinePosition endLine = lastImport.lineRange().endLine();
        FoldingRange importsRange = new FoldingRange();
        importsRange.setStartLine(strtLine.line());
        importsRange.setStartCharacter(strtLine.offset());
        importsRange.setEndLine(endLine.line());
        importsRange.setStartCharacter(endLine.offset());
```

```
        importsRange.setKind(FoldingRangeKind.Imports);

        foldingRanges.add(importsRange);
    }
    ...
}
```

Selection Range

The selection range allows the client and server to provide smart selections. Usually, the clients have key bindings to continuously select ranges. The client sends the `textDocument/selectionRange` request to the server in order to get the ranges to be selected for a given set of positions. In a simplest implementation, the servers can consider the tokens as represented in syntax trees. In more complex scenarios, the servers can consider the semantic information also, not only to select by syntax nodes but also compound statements and blocks.

Client Capabilities

Client capabilities are specified with `SelectionRangeClientCapabilities` where the `dynamicRegistration` property is set when the client supports dynamically registering the capability.

Server Capabilities

Server capabilities can be set either by setting the `boolean` flag or with `SelectionRangeOptions`, while registration options are set with the `SelectionRangeRegistrationOptions`. You can refer to `ServerInitUtils.java` for setting the server capabilities.

Generating the Response

The client sends a `SelectionRangeParams` data model as input parameters. The input parameter contains two properties. The `textDocument` property specifies the text document for which the request is initiated. The `positions` property specifies the list of positions in the text document for which the selection ranges are requested.

It is important to keep in mind that the server's response is also bound to the order of positions. For example, the second range value specified in the response is for the second position specified in the input.

As a response, the server sends a list of SelectionRange models or null. The SelectionRange contains two properties. The range property specifies the range in the document to be selected. The optional parent property specifies the parent selection range (SelectionRange) enclosing the current range.

Listing 9-7 demonstrates how to generate a selection range for the Ballerina language.

Note In VS Code, the key combination for expand selection will trigger the selection range request.

Listing 9-7. Generating the Response for selectionRange

```
public class SelectionRangeProvider extends AbstractProvider {
    public static List<SelectionRange>
    getSelectionRange(BalSelectionRangeContext context) {

        ...

        List<SelectionRange> selectionRanges = new ArrayList<>();
        for (Position position : context.positions()) {
            NonTerminalNode nodeAtPosition =
                    ContextEvaluator.nodeAtPosition(position, context);
            NonTerminalNode parent = nodeAtPosition.parent();
            SelectionRange selectionRange = new SelectionRange();
            Range range = toRange(parent.lineRange());
            selectionRange.setRange(range);
            if (parent.parent() != null) {
                SelectionRange parentSelectionRange = new SelectionRange();
                Range parentRange = toRange(parent.parent().lineRange());
                parentSelectionRange.setRange(parentRange);
                selectionRange
                .setParent(parentSelectionRange);
            }
        }
```

```
            selectionRanges.add(selectionRange);
        }
        return selectionRanges;
    }
}
```

Linked Editing Range

Consider a scripting language such as XML. In XML, for each opening tag, there is an associated closing tag or none. In scenarios where the opening and closing tags do not match, it is grammatically incorrect. So the user has to change both tags when changing a tag name. In such cases, if the client can simultaneously change a closing or opening tag name while modifying the other, that will improve the developer experience. The Language Server Protocol allows the clients and servers to facilitate this capability via the textDocument/linkedEditingRange.

The client sends the textDocument/linkedEditingRange to the server to get the related ranges to be edited together.

Client Capabilities

Client capabilities are specified with LinkedEditingRangeClientCapabilities which contains the dynamicRegistration field specifying whether the client allows the servers to dynamically register the capability.

Server Capabilities

Server capabilities and the capability registration can be done by setting the boolean flag or LinkedEditingRangeOptions or LinkedEditingRangeRegistrationOptions.

Generating the Response

The client sends the LinkedEditingRangeParams as the input containing the text document position options.

As a response, the server sends a LinkedEditingRanges model containing the following fields.

The ranges field specifies a list of ranges in the given document. It is important to make sure that the particular ranges should have identical text, identical length and are not overlapping. The optional wordPattern field specifies a regular expression describing valid word patterns for ranges. If absent, the client will use its word pattern. Setting the word pattern is useful when the server can predict tag patterns to be edited simultaneously. In the Ballerina language, we are going to demonstrate the capability for xml literals, as shown in Listing 9-8. In order to observe the behavior on VS Code, add the Ballerina source snippet shown in Listing 9-9 and keep the cursor on either of the opening or closing tags of the xml statement. Then you can see that the client colors both the starting and closing tags, and when you edit the name, it will automatically change the value of the corresponding opening or closing tag.

Listing 9-8. Generating the Response for linkedEditingRange
(LinkedEditingRangeProvider.java)

```
public static LinkedEditingRanges
getLinkedEditingRanges(BalLinkedEditingRangeContext context) {
    NonTerminalNode nodeAtCursor = context.getNodeAtCursor();
    if (nodeAtCursor.kind() != SyntaxKind.XML_SIMPLE_NAME) {
        return null;
    }
    NonTerminalNode parent = nodeAtCursor.parent();
    XMLStartTagNode startTag;
    XMLEndTagNode endTag;
    // Capture the start and the end tags
    if (parent.kind() == SyntaxKind.XML_ELEMENT_START_TAG) {
        startTag = (XMLStartTagNode) parent;
        endTag = ((XMLElementNode) parent.parent()).endTag();
    } else if (parent.kind() == SyntaxKind.XML_ELEMENT_END_TAG) {
        startTag = ((XMLElementNode) parent.parent()).startTag();
        endTag = (XMLEndTagNode) parent;
    } else {
        return null;
    }
    LinkedEditingRanges editingRanges = new LinkedEditingRanges();
    List<Range> ranges = new ArrayList<>();
```

```
    ranges.add(toRange(startTag.name().lineRange()));
    ranges.add(toRange(endTag.name().lineRange()));

    editingRanges.setRanges(ranges);
    return editingRanges;
}
```

Listing 9-9. Using xml in Ballerina

```
function testXml() returns xml {
    // Keep the cursor on book and edit
    xml xmlValue = xml `<book>The Lost World</book>`;
    return xmlValue;
}
```

Prepare Call Hierarchy

In programming languages, it is a common requirement to view the call hierarchy for function/method calls. A call hierarchy allows the developers to have a high-level glance at how a certain language construct is being called throughout the code. Not only the function/method calls but also any language construct can be represented in a call hierarchy depending on the language semantics of the programming language.

Client Capabilities

Client capabilities are specified with `CallHierarchyClientCapabilities` which contains the `dynamicRegistration` field specifying whether the client allows the servers to dynamically register the capability.

Server Capabilities

Server capabilities and the capability registration can be done by setting the `boolean` flag or `CallHierarchyOptions` or `CallHierarchyRegistrationOptions`.

Generating the Response

The client sends the `CallHierarchyPrepareParams` as the request parameters containing the positional details – the document URI and the cursor position.

The server, as a response, sends a list of `CallHierarchyItems`. The name field specifies the name of the symbol at the given position.

The `kind` field specifies the symbol kind (`SymbolKind`) such as `Variable`, `Field`, `Method`, etc.

The optional `tags` field specifies the `SymbolTags` associated with the particular symbol (the current protocol version supports the `Deprecated` tag only).

The `detail` field specifies additional details about the symbol. This information can be a short documentation description, a function signature of a given function symbol, or even the type information for the cases of field symbols.

The `uri` (`DocumentUri`) field specifies the URI of the particular symbol's definition. For example, in the case of a function call, the URI should refer to where the function definition is.

The `range` and `selectionRange` fields, respectively, refer to the range of the definition and the range of the identifier which should be highlighted upon selection.

The `data` field specifies any additional data to be preserved between the `prepareCallHierarchy` call and the `callHierarchyIncoming` and `callHierarchyOutgoing` calls. In order to extract the call hierarchy information, the servers have to extract semantic information which will be expensive for recomputing. In such cases, the server can refer to the precalculated information in between the operations saving as metadata in the `data` field.

Listing 9-10 shows generating the response for the `prepareCallHierarchy` operation.

Listing 9-10. Generating the Response for prepareCallHierarchy (CallHierarchyProvider.java)

```
public static List<CallHierarchyItem> prepare(
        BalPosBasedContext context) {

    ...

    FunctionSymbol functionSymbol = (FunctionSymbol) symbol.get();
    CallHierarchyItem cItem = new CallHierarchyItem();
    cItem.setKind(org.eclipse.lsp4j.SymbolKind.Function);
    cItem.setName(functionSymbol.getName().orElseThrow());
    //calculate start and end range
```

```
...
cItem.setRange(new Range(rStart, rEnd));

Optional<Node> funcNode = compilerManager.getNode(path, lineRange.
startLine().line(),
        lineRange.startLine().offset());
if (funcNode.isEmpty() || funcNode.get().kind() != SyntaxKind.FUNCTION_
DEFINITION) {
    return Collections.emptyList();
}
IdentifierToken fName = ((FunctionDefinitionNode) funcNode.get()).
functionName();
LineRange nameLineRange = fName.lineRange();
Position srStart = new Position(nameLineRange.startLine().line(),
nameLineRange.startLine().offset());
Position srEnd = new Position(nameLineRange.endLine().line(),
nameLineRange.endLine().offset());
Path prjRoot = compilerManager.getProjectRoot(path).orElseThrow();
String uri = getUriFromLocation(symbol.get(), symbol.get().
getLocation().get(), prjRoot);
cItem.setSelectionRange(new Range(srStart, srEnd));
cItem.setUri(uri);
/*
Necessary semantic information can
be added with data field as cItem.setData();
 */
return Collections.singletonList(cItem);
}
```

Call Hierarchy Incoming

In the previous section, we had a look at the prepareCallHierarchy operation.
The prepareCallHierarchy operation works in two steps. First, the client sends the
prepareCallHierarchy request and then sends the incomingCalls request or the
outgoingCalls request.

The client sends the `callHierarchy/incomingCalls` to the server for requesting the incoming call for a call hierarchy item. The server then has to analyze the semantic information of a symbol associated with a call hierarchy item and find all the incoming references for the symbol. For example, consider a function/method call where incoming calls are requested. The resulting incoming calls can include functions enclosing the function call expression. It's not only the functions, but also, depending on the language semantics, the server can define the granularity of the constructs. For example, in the Ballerina language, there can be top-level variable declarations referring to function call expressions, and in `TypeScript`, arrow functions can refer to function call expressions.

There are no separate client and server capabilities specified for the `callHierarchy/incomingCalls`, and the capabilities will be registered along with the `prepareCallHierarchy` capabilities.

Generating the Response

As the request parameters, the client sends `CallHierarchyIncomingCallsParams` to the server. The `item` field specifies the `CallHierarchyItem` for which the incoming calls should be calculated. The server can infer information related to the symbol such as the resource URI and metadata which is set with the data field in the `prepareCallHierarchy` response.

As a response, the server sends a list of `CallHierarchyIncomingCall` or `null`. The `from` (`CallHierarchyItem`) field in the data model specifies which item initiates the call. Also, the `fromRanges` field specifies a list of `Ranges` within the initiator where the incoming call appears. For example, consider a function definition (say fA) which we have identified as an incoming call for another function (say fB), and the `fromRanges` specifies the places where fB appears within fA (Listing 9-11). You can refer to `CallHierarchyProvider.java` for more information regarding the implementation.

Listing 9-11. Incoming Calls

```
function fA() {
    ...
    // Range appears in the fromRanges
    fB();
```

```
    if (...) {
            // Range appears in the fromRanges
            fB();
    }
      ...
}
function fB() {
      ...
}
```

Call Hierarchy Outgoing

Similar to the incoming call request, the client sends the `callHierarchy/outgoingCalls` request to the server to get outgoing calls from a particular symbol. Similar to the incoming call request, the server does not need specific registration options to register the capability since it will be registered when the server registers the `prepareCallHierarchy` capability.

Generating the Response

As the request parameters, the client sends `CallHierarchyOutgoingCallsParams` to the server. The `item` field specifies the `CallHierarchyItem` from which the outgoing calls should be calculated. The server can infer information related to the symbol such as the resource URI and metadata set with the `data` field.

As a response, the server sends a list of `CallHierarchyOutgoingCall` or null. The `to` (`CallHierarchyItem`) field in the data model specifies the call's definition (e.g., a function definition). Also, the `fromRanges` field specifies a list of Ranges. The ranges are the places where the particular `CallHierarchyItem` specified into the `field` appears. You can refer to `CallHierarchyProvider.java` for more information regarding the implementation.

Note   The prepare call hierarchy, call hierarchy incoming, and call hierarchy outgoing features are all linked together in a single user experience. In VS Code, right-click a symbol, and in the context menu, you can find the **Show Call Hierarchy** menu item which will trigger the call hierarchy features.

Summary

When it comes to the developer experience, it is not only the editing and navigation support that benefit the users. If we consider capabilities such as folding and smart selection those add a great value to the development process/developer experience of the users. Consider a CLI-based editor, and you open a document with several hundred lines with documentation and comments. In such a scenario, focusing on a specific code block is cumbersome without folding the unnecessary content. This is only a single scenario where presentation and selection features are useful, and in this chapter, we had a deep dive into folding, selection, and presentation features which are facilitated via the Language Server Protocol along with example implementations.

Up to this chapter, we had an in-depth look at language features related to a text document. In the next chapter, we are going to have a look at workspace features provided by the Language Server Protocol in detail.

CHAPTER 10

Workspace Operations

The usage of workspace operations are applicable to the current workspace instance which has been instantiated by the client. Workspace operations such as `applyEdit` and `executeCommand` are initiated by the server to be reflected on the workspace, while notifications such as `didChangeConfigurations` and `didChangeWatchedFiles` are initiated by the client. The given Language Server implementation can utilize these workspace operations to enhance the developer experience by injecting the ecosystem's knowledge to the language services.

When we consider programming languages in general, it is not only a single source file or a project directory associated with the project. There are metadata files and configuration files associated with the project. When it comes to language features such as formatting and refactoring options such as code actions, the user should be able to configure the behaviors. For example, the user should be able to configure the formatting behavior to use tabs instead of spaces for the indentation. In such scenarios, smartness providers should be able to access these configuration options.

Let's consider another example scenario. There are situations where language services initiate indexes for better performance. This indexing can be for a single project or for all the projects added to a given workspace. These two examples we discussed expose an important capability, which is the awareness of the workspace when implementing language services. The Language Server Protocol defines a wide range of workspace operations to get information about the client's workspace.

© Nadeeshaan Gunasinghe and Nipuna Marcus 2022
N. Gunasinghe and N. Marcus, *Language Server Protocol and Implementation*,
https://doi.org/10.1007/978-1-4842-7792-8_10

Workspace Folders

When it comes to editors and similar clients, it is a common feature/capability to maintain more than one project. For example, VS Code supports multiple project folders in the workspace with the multi-root workspace[1] concept. Now consider the scenario where the Language Server implements the workspace symbol, where the server has to capture all the symbols in the workspace. If there are multiple projects in the workspace, then the server has to consider all together. In order to do so, the server should capture the projects available in the workspace.

The server sends the `workspace/workspaceFolders` request to the client to get the folders in the current workspace. In earlier protocol versions, the client could access the root URI for the workspace with the `InitializeParams` sent during the initialize request, and it has been deprecated with latest versions in favor of the `workspace/workspaceFolders` operation.

Note   The multi-root workspace concept is a feature in the VS Code editor, and depending on the IDEs/editors, the feature can be different.

Client Capabilities

Client capabilities are specified with a boolean value which can be accessed via the property `workspace.workspaceFolders`.

Server Capabilities

Server capabilities are specified with `WorkspaceFoldersServerCapabilities` where the supported field is set to specify the client support. The `changeNotifications` property can be set to receive client-initiated notifications for workspace folder changes. By setting the `changeNotifications` property, the server can receive notifications such as `workspace/didChangeWorkspaceFolders` which we will be discussing in the next step. The `changeNotifications` property can either be a boolean value or a string, where the string value is considered as an ID which can be used to unregister the capability.

---

[1]https://code.visualstudio.com/docs/editor/multi-root-workspaces

Sending the Request

As a response, the client sends a list of WorkspaceFolder data models where the uri(DocumentUri) field specifies the resource URI of the folder, and the name field specifies the name of the folder.

In our example use case, we set the supported field and set the changeNotifications with a boolean value to receive change notifications. We will be looking at the usage of workspace folders in the workspace symbols' implementation.

Workspace Folders Change Notification

The client sends the workspace/didChangeWorkspaceFolders notification to the server in order to notify any folder changes (addition or removal) happening in the workspace.

In programming languages which have the multi-module project capability, it is a requirement to refresh the project/module (depending on the language semantics) upon addition or removal of new modules to the project on demand. For example, in the Ballerina language, the language specification defines a multi-module project structure,[2] and the users can refer to a module in other modules by adding an import statement and calling public constructs. During the development process, the users can add new modules and remove existing modules from time to time. In such scenarios, the user should be able to reflect these changes without restarting the IDE/editor each time. In order to handle such scenarios, the server can use the workspace/didChangeWorkspaceFolders notification and dynamically refresh in-memory project models.

In the previous section, we discussed the workspace/workspaceFolders request sent by the server to the client in order to get the current workspace's folders. In the capability registration, we observed a property changeNotifications which can be set by the server to receive workspace folder change notifications.

Note   In this example scenario we assume that the user opens a module at a time in the workspace, instead of opening the root project folder, and once a new module is added through the file system the user adds the module to the workspace manually.

---

[2]https://ballerina.io/learn/user-guide/ballerina-packages/modules/

Client Capabilities

There are no specific client capabilities defined for the notification, and the client capability is inferred through the workspaceFolders registration options.

Server Capabilities

In the previous section, we discussed the workspaceFolders request sent by the server to the client in order to get the current workspace's folders. In the capability registration, we observed a property changeNotifications which can be set by the server to receive workspace folder change notifications.

Processing the Notification

The client sends the DidChangeWorkspaceFoldersParams data model as the notification parameters which contains the event property which is a WorkspaceFoldersChangeEvent containing two properties added and removed. Those properties represent the added and removed folders in the workspace associated with the notification.

Listing 10-1 shows reloading the in-memory Ballerina project instance when the server receives the didChangeWorkspaceFolders notification.

Listing 10-1. Reload the Ballerina Project on Workspace Folder Changes (WSFolderChangeHandler.java)

```
public static void updateProjects(BalWorkspaceContext context,
                                  DidChangeWorkspaceFoldersParams params) {
    CompilerManager cManager = context.compilerManager();
    WorkspaceFoldersChangeEvent event = params.getEvent();
    List<WorkspaceFolder> modifiedFolders =
            Stream.concat(event.getAdded().stream(),
            event.getRemoved().stream()).collect(Collectors.toList());
    List<Path> reloadedProjects = new ArrayList<>();
    for (WorkspaceFolder folder : modifiedFolders) {
        Path path = CommonUtils.uriToPath(folder.getUri());
        Optional<Path> projectRoot = cManager.getProjectRoot(path);
```

```
    if (projectRoot.isEmpty()
            || reloadedProjects.contains(projectRoot.get())) {
        continue;
    }
    Optional<Project> project =
            cManager.getProject(projectRoot.get());
    if (project.isEmpty()) {
        continue;
    }
    // If folder is added, then reload the project instance
    cManager.reloadProject(projectRoot.get());
    reloadedProjects.add(projectRoot.get());
  }
}
```

Reloading project instances is one of the use cases which we can implement upon receiving the workspace/didChangeWorkspaceFolders notification. Another such use case is recalculating indexes maintained in the server side. We have demonstrated how to achieve the use case along with the progress reporting capability, which we will be looking at in Chapter 11.

Depending on the compiler APIs and in-memory project models, partially updating the project or reloading the project can be different from one programming language to another. In either of the cases, with the modification of the source structure of projects, the user should be able to immediately experience the modified semantics.

Notification of Configuration Change

When implementing a plugin, there are various configurations the plugin developer includes for a better developer experience. It is not only plugin configurations, but also there are certain default configurations associated with the tool itself. When implementing the Language Server, the server can dynamically change the behavior/ internal state based on these configuration changes. In our example, we are going to show how the Language Server is going to dynamically enable and disable a code action upon the configuration changes.

The Language Server Protocol allows the client to send notifications for client configuration changes to the server with the workspace/didChangeConfiguration notification. The server can use this notification to extract the desired configuration values and make internal decisions.

Client Capabilities

Client capabilities are specified with the DidChangeConfigurationClientCapabilities model which contains the dynamicRegistration property which allows the server to dynamically register the capability.

Processing the Notification

The client notification is sent with the DidChangeConfigurationParams data model. Configuration settings are specified in the settings property. The server then needs to extract the particular configuration from the JSON data model and process.

It is important that both the client and the server have to be in agreement regarding the configuration values which are going to be utilized. For example, user settings can be similar between clients, but when we consider a custom configuration such as in our example we are going to look at next, the client also has to add the particular configuration value in the client implementation depending on the Language Server implementation it is going to support.

The client implementation contains the ballerina.codeAction.documentation user setting for the VS Code client's package.json configuration file for enabling and disabling the documentation code action. Listing 10-2 shows that the server updates a singleton config holder instance upon the notification which will be reflected to the server instance, and Listing 10-3 shows how the modified code action provider reads the configuration value and decides whether to show the documentation code action or not. Listing 10-4 shows how the server's configuration holder implementation accesses the particular configuration value. It is important to know that the main reason behind exposing the configuration options as an interface (ConfigurationHolder.java) is to avoid code duplication and make the development smoother.

Listing 10-2. Update the Configuration Holder (BalWorkspaceService.java)

```java
public void didChangeConfiguration(
        DidChangeConfigurationParams params) {
    JsonObject settings = (JsonObject) params.getSettings();
    JsonElement configSection =
            settings.get(ConfigurationHolder.CONFIG_SECTION);
    if (configSection != null) {
        ConfigurationHolder.getInstance().update(configSection);
    }
}
```

Listing 10-3. Conditionally Get the Documentation Code Action
(CodeActionProvider.java)

```java
public static List<Either<Command, CodeAction>>
getCodeAction(BalCodeActionContext context, CodeActionParams params) {
    ...
    ConfigurationHolder configHolder = context.clientConfigHolder();
    if (topLevelNode.isPresent() && topLevelNode.get().kind()
            == SyntaxKind.FUNCTION_DEFINITION
            && configHolder.isDocumentationCodeActionEnabled()) {
        codeActions.add(getAddDocsCodeAction(context,
                params,
                topLevelNode.get())
        );
    }

    return codeActions;
}
```

Listing 10-4. Accessing the Configuration Options (ConfigurationHolderImpl.java)

```java
public class ConfigurationHolderImpl implements ConfigurationHolder {
    ...
    public boolean isDocumentationCodeActionEnabled() {
```

```
    if (this.config == null) {
        return false;
    }

    return ((JsonObject) this.config)
            .get("codeAction")
  .getAsJsonObject()
  .get("documentation").getAsBoolean();
    }
}
```

In order to send configuration change notifications to the server, on the client side we have to add the configuration as shown in Listing 10-5.

Listing 10-5. Add the Ballerina Configuration Section to Send with didChangeConfiguration

```
let clientOptions: LanguageClientOptions = {
        // Register the server for ballerina documents
        documentSelector:
        [{ scheme: 'file', language: 'ballerina' }],
        initializationOptions: {
                    enableDocumentationCodeLenses: false,
        },
        // Add the ballerina configuration section
        synchronize: { configurationSection: ['ballerina'] },
        outputChannel: logChannel
};
```

It is important to keep in mind that the server can decide whether to dynamically update a configuration holder implementation or to request configuration values from the client whenever necessary. The Language Server Protocol facilitates this behavior with the workspace/configuration request which is initiated by the server. In the next section, we will be looking into this request in detail.

Note   In VS Code, the settings synchronization model has been deprecated in favor of the pull model we are going to discuss later.

Configuration

In the previous section, we looked at how to dynamically make runtime decisions immediately when client configurations are changed. For that, we utilized the `workspace/didChangeConfiguration` operation. Other than this, the Language Server Protocol allows the server to pull the configurations from the client. It is the server implementation's decision to choose which method of configuration access is to be used. Say that the server heavily depends on the configurations to implement the code completion feature. For example, the server implementation can generate a specific set of code snippets depending on a configuration value. The frequency of the code completion operation is higher when compared to other operations during the development process. Hence, it is not a viable solution to pull the configurations from the client for each completion trigger. Likewise, the server should not depend on the configuration pull for operations with higher execution frequency.

The Language Server Protocol allows the server to fetch the configuration on demand by sending the `workspace/configuration` request to the client to get the client configurations.

Client Capabilities

Client capabilities are specified with a boolean value in the `workspace.configuration` property.

Generating the Request

The server can request multiple configurations in a single request. Also, the server can specify the configuration combination it wants to request. As the request parameters, the server sends a list of `ConfigurationParams` to the client. The `ConfigurationParams` includes the `items` property which holds a list of `ConfigurationItems`. A given `ConfigurationItem` specifies a combination for a configuration. The client responds with a list of configurations, and the order of configurations is the same as the order of items sent in the request. For example, the third configuration item in the response is for the third item in the request.

The `ConfigurationItem` contains two properties. The `section` property specifies which configuration section needs to be extracted. The section is represented with dot-separated values. For example, if the server wants to get the documentation code action configuration, the server can ask for the `ballerina.codeAction.documentation`. The `scopeUri` specifies a `DocumentUri` which specifies the configuration scope. For example, the clients allow the developers to define configurations for various file patterns. When we consider programming languages, there can be multiple file types. In the Ballerina language, Ballerina source files are specified with the .bal extension, and toml configuration files are used for meta-information such as Ballerina.toml and Dependencies.toml. The user can define formatting settings differently for conventional toml configurations and Ballerina.toml configurations. With the scopeUri, the server can specifically get configurations for the Ballerina.toml.

Listing 10-6 shows requesting the documentation code action configuration from the client.

Listing 10-6. Get the Documentation Code Action Configuration (CodeActionProvider.java)

```
private static boolean documentationEnabled(BalCodeActionContext context)
{
    LanguageClient client = context.getClient();
    ConfigurationParams params = new ConfigurationParams();
    ConfigurationItem item = new ConfigurationItem();
    item.setSection("ballerina.codeAction.documentation");
    params.setItems(Collections.singletonList(item));
    CompletableFuture<List<Object>> configuration =
        client.configuration(params);
    List<Object> configValue;
    try {
        configValue = configuration.get();
    } catch (InterruptedException | ExecutionException e) {
        return false;
    }
    return GSON.toJsonTree(configValue.get(0)).getAsBoolean();
}
```

Watched Files Change Notification

In Chapter 7, we discussed the workspace/codeLens/refresh operation where the server sends the particular request to the server for recalculating code lenses. As we mentioned, the trigger point to the refresh can be defined on project-level configuration changes. For example, in the Ballerina language, a change to `Ballerina.toml` configurations can lead to a project reload, and that can lead to refreshing of code lenses.

Now, if we consider the trigger point we discussed here, it is a file change event which triggers both operations' initiation. For the server to support these types of features, one of the options is to register a file system watcher for the server itself. This is not a scalable design when we consider the client's point of view. Usually, the clients have more than one extension/plugin running, and if there are multiple file watchers running, that is going to consume a considerable amount of system resources. In order to avoid this, the best option would be to have a single file watcher running and let the server implementations be notified. The Language Server Protocol fulfills this requirement with the `workspace/didChangeWatchedFiles` notification. The server implementation can register for file change events, and the client sends notification events for the respective registered event.

Client Capabilities

Client capabilities are specified with `DidChangeWatchedFilesClientCapabilities` which contains the `dynamicRegistration` property specifying whether the client supports dynamically registering the capability.

Registration Options

The server does not specify a specific server capability. Instead, the server can register for file change events. The registration options are specified with `DidChangeWatchedFilesRegistrationOptions` which contains the `watchers` property specifying a list of `FileSystemWatchers`. The `FileSystemWatcher` contains two properties.

The optional `kind` property specifies the type of event to be received for the particular file pattern. There are three `WatchKinds` defined as `Create`, `Change`, and `Delete` which are assigned the integer values 1, 2, and 4, respectively. The value associated with the kind property is a sum of the integer values specified for the `WatchKind`. For example, if the server wishes to receive `Change` and `Delete` notifications for a file, then the kind is 6 (2 + 4). If none is specified, the client assumes the kind value to be default which is 7 (1 + 2 + 4), where all three events will be received.

The globPattern property specifies the file pattern to match the files which are files that the server wishes to receive notifications for. The file pattern is specified with the glob pattern syntax, and you can read more on the glob pattern syntax from this blog[3] and from the Language Server Protocol specification[4] itself.

Listing 10-7 shows how we register a file watcher for the Ballerina.toml configuration file.

Listing 10-7. Register a File Watcher for Ballerina.toml (BalLanguageServer.java)

```java
public void initialized(InitializedParams params) {
    // Registering the onTypeFormatting capability
    ...
    // Register file watchers
    List<FileSystemWatcher> watchers = new ArrayList<>();
    watchers.add(new FileSystemWatcher("/**/"
            + ProjectConstants.BALLERINA_TOML,
            WatchKind.Create + WatchKind.Delete));
    DidChangeWatchedFilesRegistrationOptions opts =
            new DidChangeWatchedFilesRegistrationOptions(watchers);
    Registration registration =
            new Registration(UUID.randomUUID().toString(),
            "workspace/didChangeWatchedFiles", opts);
    this.client.registerCapability(
            new RegistrationParams(Collections.
            singletonList(registration)));
}
```

Processing the Notification

The client sends the DidChangeWatchedFilesParams as the notification parameters for a file event. The DidChangeWatchedFilesParams contains the changes property which specifies a list of FileEvents. Each FileEvent contains two properties as uri specifying

---

[3] https://mincong.io/2019/04/16/glob-expression-understanding/
[4] https://microsoft.github.io/language-server-protocol/specifications/
 specification-3-16/#workspace_didChangeWatchedFiles

the DocumentUri associated with the file where the event occurred and the type property which specifies the FileChangeType (Created, Changed, Deleted).

In our example (Listing 10-8), we are going to receive notifications associated with Ballerina.toml configuration files, and then we reload the in-memory project instance and send a workspace/codeLens/refresh request to the client in order to refresh code lenses.

Listing 10-8. Handle the Ballerina.toml File Create/Delete (BalWorkspaceService.java)

```java
public void didChangeWatchedFiles(DidChangeWatchedFilesParams params) {
    BalWorkspaceContext context =
            ContextBuilder.getWorkspaceContext(this.lsServerContext);
    Optional<FileEvent> ballerinaTomlEvent = params.getChanges().stream()
            .filter(fileEvent -> fileEvent.getUri().endsWith(TOML_CONFIG)
                    && fileEvent.getType() == FileChangeType.Changed)
            .findAny();

    if (ballerinaTomlEvent.isPresent()) {
        Path path = CommonUtils.uriToPath(tomlEvent.get().getUri());
        Optional<Path> projectRoot =
                context.compilerManager().getProjectRoot(path);
        if (projectRoot.isEmpty()) {
            return;
        }
        // Reload the project
        context.compilerManager().reloadProject(projectRoot.get());
        // Send codelens refresh request to client
        LanguageClient client = this.lsServerContext.getClient();
        client.refreshCodeLenses();
    }
    ...
}
```

Workspace Symbol

The client sends the `workspace/symbol` request to the server for workspace-wide symbols. When the client sends this request, it does not send any project-specific detail to locate/identify the project at the server. If the server needs to send all the symbols for the projects opened in the current workspace, the server will have to find a mechanism to identify the projects opened in the current workspace. Fortunately, we can achieve this requirement in combination with the `workspace/workspaceFolders` request we discussed at the beginning of this chapter. In the example, we will be looking at this in detail.

When implementing workspace symbols, it is important to keep in mind the performance impact of this operation. It is true that this particular operation will not be having a high usage frequency compared to features such as auto-completions. Even though the frequency is low, this operation can still take some time to complete and lead to frustration of the users. Therefore, the servers will have to think of other associated mechanisms such as indexing and caching implementations. One such concept is index-while-building.[5] Also, if you consider the Language Server's operation life cycle, it is clear that semantic models are being built for sources/projects in different locations such as auto-completions, references, and definitions. If the server implementation can implement a dynamic indexing mechanism to index symbols from built semantic models, the response time taken for operations such as `workspace/symbol` can be improved.

Client Capabilities

Client capabilities are represented by `WorkspaceSymbolClientCapabilities`.

The `dynamicRegistration` property specifies whether the client supports dynamically registering the capability.

The optional `symbolKind` property specifies the supported `SymbolKinds` by the client. The list of supported symbol kinds can be accessed with the `symbolKind.valueSet`. `SymbolKinds` are as we discussed earlier with `textDocument/documentSymbol` in Chapter 8.

---

[5] `https://docs.google.com/document/d/1cH2sTpgSnJZCkZtJl1aY-rzy4uGPcrI-6RrUpdATO2Q/edit`

The tagSupport property specifies the list of tags supported by the client. The list of supported SymbolTags can be accessed with the tagSupport.valueSet. The current protocol only supports the deprecated tag.

Server Capabilities and Registration Options

Server capabilities are specified with WorkspaceSymbolOptions, and registration options are specified with the WorkspaceSymbolRegistrationOptions. You can refer to ServerInitUtils.java to see the server capability setting and DynamicCapabilitySetter.java to observe how the dynamic capability registration is done for each operation.

Generating the Response

The client sends DocumentSymbolParams as the request parameters which includes the query property. The query property is a string which is to be used for filtering symbols.

As a response, the server sends a list of SymbolInformations. As we discussed in Chapter 8, a SymbolInformation is a flat representation of symbols with no hierarchical information representation.

In our example implementation, we are going to use a combination of operations to generate the response. We are going to use the workspace/workspaceFolders request to get the workspace folders from the client and determine the project roots and then get the symbols in each module.

As a response, the server is supposed to send all the symbols in the workspace regardless of the scoping and the visibility. However, in our implementation, for the purpose of simplification we will be using the Ballerina's semantic API to get the top-level symbols of each of the modules. Even though the example implementation is being simplified, the underlying concept is extensible.

Listing 10-9 shows the example implementation for workspace symbols.

Listing 10-9. Workspace Symbol Implementation

```
public CompletableFuture<List<? extends SymbolInformation>>
symbol(WorkspaceSymbolParams params) {
    return CompletableFuture.supplyAsync(() -> {
        BalWorkspaceContext context =
            ContextBuilder.getWorkspaceContext(this.lsServerContext);
```

```
      List<SymbolInformation> wsSymbols = new ArrayList<>();
      try {
        List<Path> projectRoots = this.getProjectRoots(context);
        for (Path projectRoot : projectRoots) {
          List<SemanticModel> semanticModels =
              context.compilerManager()
                  .getSemanticModels(projectRoot);
          for (SemanticModel semanticModel : semanticModels) {
            List<SymbolInformation> symbols =
                semanticModel.moduleSymbols().stream()
                    .filter(s -> s.getName().isPresent())
                    .map(symbol -> CommonUtils
                        .getSymbolInformation(symbol, context, projectRoot))
                    .collect(Collectors.toList());
            wsSymbols.addAll(symbols);
          }
        }
      } catch (ExecutionException | InterruptedException e) {
        // Ignore
      }
      return wsSymbols;
    });
}
// Get the project roots from workspace/workspaceFolders
private List<Path> getProjectRoots(BalWorkspaceContext context)
    throws ExecutionException, InterruptedException {
  LanguageClient client = this.lsServerContext.getClient();
  // Invoke the workspace/workspaceFolders
  CompletableFuture<List<WorkspaceFolder>> result
      = client.workspaceFolders();
  List<Path> projects = new ArrayList<>();
  for (WorkspaceFolder workspaceFolder : result.get()) {
    Path path = CommonUtils.uriToPath(workspaceFolder.getUri())
        .resolve("Ballerina.toml");
    // Ballerina project contains a Ballerina.toml
```

```
  if (!path.toFile().exists()) {
    continue;
  }
  Optional<Path> project =
      context.compilerManager().getProjectRoot(path);
  project.ifPresent(projects::add);
}
return projects;
}
```

Execute Command

In Chapter 7, we discussed the textDocument/CodeAction operation. As one of the response options to the code action requests, the server can send Commands. When the user selects one of the code actions to be executed, the client sends the workspace/executeCommand request to the server. As we mentioned during the code action implementation, the server registers the supported list of commands during the server initialization. When the server receives the executeCommand request, it is a common use case to apply a refactoring to the source code. For example, consider the Create Variable code action, and upon the command execution, the server creates a refactoring with a variable and applies a WorkspaceEdit to the source. This is achieved with the workspace/applyEdit request sent by the server to the client for carrying out a set of edits on the workspace, which we will be discussing in the next section.

Client Capabilities

Client capabilities are specified with ExecuteCommandClientCapabilities which contains the dynamicRegistration property which specifies whether the client allows to dynamically register the capability.

Server Capabilities

Server capabilities are specified with the ExecuteCommandOptions where the commands property specifies a list of commands supported by the server. In our example implementation, we register the available commands in the ServerInitUtils. getExecuteCommandOptions method.

Executing the Command

The client sends the `ExecuteCommandParams` as the request parameters. The `ExecuteCommandParams` contains two properties.

The `command` property specifies the command name that is to be executed which is one of the commands we set at the capability registration.

The `arguments` field specifies a list of arguments associated with the command. Let's consider the `Create Variable` code action. As we described in Chapter 7, we set the arguments as shown in Listing 7-11. There we hold the arguments in a `CreateVariableArgs` instance. When the user selects the particular code action to be executed and when the server receives the `executeCommand` request to be executed, the particular arguments we set with the code action will be available with the arguments of `ExecuteCommandParams`.

As a response, the server can send `any` or `null`. Even though the protocol defines a response to the request, the most common flow is that the server applies a workspace edit as mentioned earlier. Let's have a look at applying the workspace edit for the command in the next section on `workspace/applyEdit`.

Apply Edit

The `workspace/applyEdit` request is sent from the server to the client requesting to modify resources. In the previous section, we discussed one of the scenarios where the server can initiate the `applyEdit` along with a command execution. Other than that, depending on the use case the server can initiate an `applyEdit`. The particular edit operation is not limited to editing a source file. The capability allows the servers to carry out file operations such as create, rename, and delete as well. For use cases such as generating test cases, the file creation edit option can be used. If we consider a programming language such as Java, we make the file name and the class name the same. In this scenario, when a user renames a class name, the editor can rename the associated file name as well. This is another use case where we can use the apply edit capability.

Client Capabilities

Client capabilities are specified with the `workspace.applyEdit` property. It is not only the `applyEdit` client capability that is in relation with the request, but also the `WorkspaceEditClientCapabilities` has to be focused on which specifies workspace capabilities. Now, let's have a look at the workspace edit capabilities and the associated properties.

The `documentChanges` specifies whether the client supports the versioned document changes. This is an important property because the `WorkspaceEdit` data model contains two properties to specify the actual edit as the `changes` property and the `documentChanges` property which we will be discussing later in this section. The client honors the `WorkspaceEdit.documentChanges` property only if the `documentChanges` property is set to true.

The `resourceOperations` (`ResourceOperationKind`) property specifies the resource operations supported by the client, such as `Create`, `Delete`, and `Rename` of files and folders. The protocol itself specifies that the clients should at least support `Create`, `Delete`, and `Rename` of files and folders. This is a very useful feature for scenarios such as generating files and folders via code action execution. For example, consider a scenario where the server provides a code action to generate test cases for public functions where the server can create new files with test cases.

The `failureHandling` (`FailureHandlingKind`) property specifies the types of failure handling supported by the client. The current protocol supports `Abort`, `Transactional`, `TextOnlyTransactional`, and `Undo`:

- Abort – Applying the edit fails since one of the changes failed. Edits applied before and after the particular failure will remain executed.

- Transactional – Edits which were carried out transactionally have been failed.

- TextOnlyTransactional – If the workspace edit contains only textual file changes they are executed transactionally. If the changes include resource changes such as delete, create, and rename, then upon a failure the failure handling would be TextOnlyTransactional.

- Undo – The client trying to undo an already executed edit and being failed doing so.

Note   When the server receives the response for the applyEdit operation, the response contains the FailureHandlingKind, if there is any. Then the server can use this information to properly log the errors and notify the users with notifications.

The normalizesLineEndings specifies whether the client normalizes/modifies the line endings in the workspace edit to a client-specific value. For example, the client can always convert the line endings to \n without considering the system preferences.

The changeAnnotationSupport specifies whether the client supports change annotations for text edits, create file, delete file, and rename file. We discussed one of the usages of annotated text edits in Chapter 7 with the textDocument/rename operation.

Sending the Request

The server sends workspace/applyEdit with the ApplyWorkspaceEditParams as the request parameters which contains two properties.

The label property specifies a string label which is used to be shown in the user interface. One of the most common use case is to be shown on an undo-redo stack.

The edit property specifies the actual edits (WorkspaceEdit) to be applied with the request.

Listing 10-10 shows an example use case where we apply a workspace edit for the Create Variable command execution which we discussed in the previous section.

Listing 10-10. WorkspaceEdit for Create Variable Command Execution (BalWorkspaceService.java)

```
private ApplyWorkspaceEditResponse
applyCreateVarWorkspaceEdit(BalWorkspaceContext context,
            ExecuteCommandParams params) {
  JsonObject arg = (JsonObject) params.getArguments().get(0);
  CommandArgument commandArg = new Gson().fromJson(arg,
  CommandArgument.class);
  if (!commandArg.getKey().equals("params")) {
    return null;
  }
```

```
CreateVariableArgs createVarArgs = commandArg.
getValue(CreateVariableArgs.class);
WorkspaceEdit workspaceEdit = new WorkspaceEdit();
TextDocumentEdit documentEdit = new TextDocumentEdit();
VersionedTextDocumentIdentifier identifier =
    new VersionedTextDocumentIdentifier();
identifier.setUri(createVarArgs.getUri());
TextEdit textEdit = new TextEdit(createVarArgs.getRange(),
    createVarArgs.getNewText());
documentEdit.setEdits(Collections.singletonList(textEdit));
documentEdit.setTextDocument(identifier);
Either<TextDocumentEdit, ResourceOperation> documentChanges =
    Either.forLeft(documentEdit);
workspaceEdit.setDocumentChanges(Collections.singletonList(documentChanges));
ApplyWorkspaceEditParams applyEditParams = new ApplyWorkspaceEditParams();
applyEditParams.setEdit(workspaceEdit);
CompletableFuture<ApplyWorkspaceEditResponse> response =
    context.getClient().applyEdit(applyEditParams);
try {
  return response.get();
} catch (InterruptedException | ExecutionException e) {
  // Handle gracefully
}
return null;
}
```

Will Create Files

Throughout the chapters, we discussed workspace edits which can be used by the
server to create files, rename files, and delete files as well. Other than that, there are
scenarios where the client generates new files, rename and delete. Consider the VS Code
commands which allow the user to execute various operations on the workspace. For
example, the client can provide an option to create meta files on demand via executing
commands, which are not initiated by the server. When such meta files are generated,

the server will need to get notified for housekeeping tasks such as cleaning caches and reloading project instances.

The client sends the `workspace/willCreateFiles` request to the server when a file is created which is initiated via the client. At the time when the server receives the request, the particular file has not been created in the file system. If we consider an example of creating a meta file, the server can reply with a `WorkspaceEdit`, to apply for the workspace, in order to clear cached files. It is important to note that the client will drop the workspace edits if calculating the edit is taking time. This is to ensure a smooth file creation with a noticeable delay.

Client Capabilities

Client capabilities are specified with `workspace.fileOperations.willCreate`, which is a boolean flag.

Registration Options

The registration options are specified with `FileOperationRegistrationOptions` which contains the `filters` property which specifies a list of `FileOperationFilters`.

A given filter specified with the `FileOperationFilter` data model contains two properties. The `scheme` property specifies a URI scheme such as `file/untitled`, and the `pattern` property specifies a `FileOperationPattern` data model. For a detailed description and usage of the registration options, refer to `ServerInitUtils.java`.

Generating the Response

The client sends the `workspace/willCreateFiles` request with `CreateFilesParams` which contains the `files` property specifying a list of `FileCreates` with the respective URIs.

As a response, the server can either send a `WorkspaceEdit` or `null`. We discussed in the previous sections how to create a workspace edit, and the concepts and best practices discussed throughout the chapters apply to this case as well. Since most of the concepts are similar to the ones we discussed earlier, you can refer to `FileOperationEventsHandler.java`.

Did Create Files

In the previous section, we discussed the `workspace/willCreateFiles` request sent by the client to the server. The `workspace/didCreateFiles` notification is sent by the client to notify a file creation event after the actual file is created on the system. We discussed in the previous section on carrying out pre-housekeeping tasks before the file creation.

For example, consider creating a configuration file such as `Ballerina.toml`, and the server can add a default content to the file. The server can initiate the associated workspace edit upon receiving the `didCreateFiles` notification. Depending on the requirement, it is not only file editing, but also the server can apply edits to restructure or create directory structures.

Client Capabilities

Client capabilities are specified with the `workspace.fileOperations.didCreate` boolean flag.

Server Capabilities

As discussed in the previous section, we can set the server capabilities via the `FileOperationRegistrationOptions` by setting the `workspace.fileOperations.didCreate` property.

Handling the Notification

The server sends the `workspace/didCreateFiles` notification with `CreateFilesParams` as the input parameter. Since most of the concepts are similar to the ones we discussed earlier, you can refer to `FileOperationEventsHandler.java` for an example implementation.

Will Rename Files

Similar to the `workspace/willCreateFiles` request, the client sends the `workspace/willRenameFiles` before renaming the files, where the renaming is initiated by the client. As discussed in the `willCreateFiles` operation, the server can respond with `WorkspaceEdit` or `null`.

Client Capabilities

Client capabilities are specified with the `workspace.fileOperations.willRename` boolean flag.

Server Capabilities

Similar to what we discussed in earlier sections, we can set the server capabilities via the `FileOperationRegistrationOptions` by setting the `workspace.fileOperations.willRename` property.

Generating the Response

The client sends the `workspace/willRenameFiles` with `RenameFilesParams` with the `files` property which specifies the list of files to be renamed. The file to be renamed is specified with the `FileRename` data model. The two properties, `oldUri` and `newUri`, respectively, specify the file URI before renaming and after renaming.

Since most of the concepts are similar to the ones we discussed earlier, you can refer to `FileOperationEventsHandler.java` for an example implementation.

Did Rename Files

For example, consider Java where class names can be associated with file names. If you rename one of the source files, how convenient it would be for the user to refactor the associated class name as well as the associated references of the particular class. This use case can be implemented by considering the `workspace/didRenameFiles` notification sent by the client as a trigger.

Client Capabilities

Client capabilities are specified with the `workspace.fileOperations.didRename` boolean flag.

Server Capabilities

As discussed in the previous section, we can set the server capabilities via the `FileOperationRegistrationOptions` by setting the `workspace.fileOperations.didRename` property.

Handling the Notification

The server sends the `workspace/didRenameFiles` notification with `RenameFilesParams` as the input parameter. Since most of the concepts are similar to the ones we discussed earlier, you can refer to `FileOperationEventsHandler.java` for an example implementation.

Will Delete Files

Similar to the `workspace/willCreateFiles` request, the client sends the `workspace/willDeleteFiles` before deleting the files, where the deleting is initiated by the client. As discussed in the `willCreateFiles` operation, the server can respond with `WorkspaceEdit` or `null`.

Consider that the server implementation has registered file watchers for a specific file or the server implementation has reference indexes registered for a particular file. Upon the request, the server can initiate resource freeing such as unregistering file watchers.

Client Capabilities

Client capabilities are specified with the `workspace.fileOperations.willDelete` boolean flag.

Server Capabilities

Similar to what we discussed in earlier sections, we can set the server capabilities via the `FileOperationRegistrationOptions` by setting the `workspace.fileOperations.willDelete` property.

Generating the Response

The client sends the `workspace/willDeleteFiles` with `DeleteFilesParams` with the `files` property which specifies the list of files to be deleted. The file to be deleted is specified with the `FileDelete` data model where the `uri` property specifies the file URI which is going to be deleted.

Since most of the concepts are similar to the ones we discussed earlier, you can refer to `FileOperationEventsHandler.java` for an example implementation.

Deleted Files Notification

For example, consider in Ballerina, the user might delete the Ballerina.toml file from the package, leading the sources within the package to become single file projects. In such a case, the server needs to provide diagnostics by recomputing semantic models for individual sources as well as removing/invalidating old in-memory models for the package. This use case can be implemented by considering the `workspace/didDeleteFiles` notification sent by the client as a trigger.

Client Capabilities

Client capabilities are specified with the `workspace.fileOperations.didDelete` boolean flag.

Server Capabilities

As discussed in the previous section, we can set the server capabilities via the `FileOperationRegistrationOptions` by setting the `workspace.fileOperations.didDelete` property.

Handling the Notification

The server sends the `workspace/didDeleteFiles` notification with `DeleteFilesParams` as the input parameter. Since most of the concepts are similar to the ones we discussed earlier, you can refer to `FileOperationEventsHandler.java` for an example implementation.

Summary

In this chapter, we had a detailed look at workspace operations associated with the Language Server Protocol along with example implementations as well as use cases. Workspace operations are not only limited to a single documentation or for text documents in the workspace. The capabilities described in this chapter are associated with the editor's workspace, and the server can improve the developer experience by combining the operations together. For example, the `WorkspaceEdits` can be combined with file event operations as well as command executions.

With workspace operations, the server is allowed to take extra steps to get the workspace knowledge to the server and incorporate project-wide/workspace-wide intelligence to the Language Server implementation, allowing the developer to have a smoother developer experience.

Up to this chapter, we looked at the text document and workspace capabilities provided by the Language Server Protocol. Since we have a good understanding of the fundamental concepts, it's time to have a look at advanced use cases and how to leverage Language Server features to implement them. In the next chapter, we are going to look at advanced use cases where we can enhance the default capabilities.

CHAPTER 11

Advanced Concepts

In the previous chapters, we looked at the general operations and their usages when it comes to real-world use cases' implementations. Other than the general operations, we are going to look at some advanced concepts in the Language Server Protocol.

In IDEs, you have seen that there are mechanisms to provide users various progress notifications continuously as well as from time to time. Earlier, we looked at how we can use notifications, and in this chapter, we will look at progress notifications.

The Language Server Protocol can be extended in many ways. Depending on the requirements, the server developers can provide different extension points allowing third parties who use the Language Server to write extensions to expand Language Server capabilities. We will be looking into some extension points, and the developers can use the same concepts to introduce more extension points.

Work Done Progress

When using IDEs and text editors, you might have seen that there are different background tasks running such as indexing, building, downloading dependencies, and so on. Not only that, but also there are situations where the server takes some time to respond to certain operations such as finding references within the project. Even in those scenarios, the server can send work done progress notifications to the client for displaying the progress to the users.

When it comes to progress reporting, one important factor we need to consider is the parallel processing of these notifications. For example, let's consider that the server has two tasks to be carried out which are downloading the dependencies and indexing the project. If we consider this scenario carefully, the project index also captures the dependencies of the project for indexing. Therefore, running both these tasks in parallel can introduce inconsistencies in the project index. In such scenarios, the server should decide the order of tasks to be run.

© Nadeeshaan Gunasinghe and Nipuna Marcus 2022
N. Gunasinghe and N. Marcus, *Language Server Protocol and Implementation*,
https://doi.org/10.1007/978-1-4842-7792-8_11

The progress is reported with the $/progress notification. There are three forms of the notification which is distinguished by the payload we send with the notification which we will be looking at later. The protocol defines two different ways for progress initiation:

1. Client-initiated progress reporting

2. Server-initiated progress reporting

In either of the options, progress reporting is correlated with a generated token. In earlier chapters, we had a look at various language features and capabilities. For example, let's consider the completion and reference support. In both of the language features, you can observe in the server capabilities that the server can set the workDoneProgress property. Also, at the client capabilities, the client specifies the support for the workDoneProgress capability. Listings 11-1 and 11-2 are trace logs extracted from the server initialization and respectively show the client and server capabilities for the progress support.

Listing 11-1. Server Capabilities for WorkDoneProgress

```
"capabilities": {
    ...
        "completionProvider": {
            "resolveProvider": true,
            "triggerCharacters": [
                ".",
                ">"
            ],
            "workDoneProgress": true
        }
        ...
}
```

Listing 11-2. Completion Capability for WorkDoneProgress

```
{
    ...
    "capabilities": {
        "window": {
            "showMessage": {
                "messageActionItem": {
```

212

```
                "additionalPropertiesSupport": true
            }
        },
        "showDocument": {
            "support": true
        },
        "workDoneProgress": true
    }
}
...
}
```

It is important to note that the workDoneProgress property set in the client capabilities specifies that the client allows server-initiated progress support. If the client allows progress support for the requests, which is the client-initiated progress reporting, it is notified to the server with the request parameters itself. For example, if you consider the auto-completion request and the client supports progress reporting for the textDocument/completions request, the request parameters will look like in Listing 11-3 where you can see the workDoneToken property. This token is used by the server to notify the progress for the particular request.

Listing 11-3. Client-Initiated WorkDoneProgress Support for Auto-completions

```
{
    "textDocument": {
        "uri": ".../testSource.bal"
    },
    "position": {
        "line": 2,
        "character": 6
    },
    "context": {
        "includeDeclaration": true
    }
    "workDoneToken": "7cb966ba-cb4f-11eb-b8bc-0242ac130003"
}
```

For server-initiated progress reporting, it is the server that generates the workDoneToken in the first place, and then onward the particular token is used for reporting the progress.

In our example, we are going to look at server-initiated progress reporting, and the same concepts can be applied to client-initiated progress reporting as well. In our example, when we get the workspace/didChangeWorkspaceFolders notification, we are going to run an indexing task to cache all the module symbols in the workspace. Let's have a look at the data models associated with each of the states along with the implementation.

Begin Progress

The server initiates the progress with the progress begin notification. The progress begin is notified with the $/progress notification and the WorkDoneProgressBegin payload which is used for distinguishing from other progress notification types such as reporting and end. The WorkDoneProgressBegin data model contains the following properties.

The kind property specifies the progress notification kind. As mentioned earlier, progress notifications do not have specific notifications for each progress kind. For the progress begin notification, the kind value is begin.

The title property specifies the title to be shown on the UI when showing the progress bar. In our use case, we will set the title to Indexing Workspace.

The cancellable property specifies whether the server allows to cancel the running operation. The client will show a cancel icon for the user to cancel the operation. The cancellable property is also set with the WorkDoneProgressReport data model which we will discuss next.

The optional message property specifies a string, which is for notifying the progress such as a status update. During the begin notification, the server can set the initial status, for example, 1 of 3 projects are indexing. We will discuss next that the message property is also available with the WorkDoneProgressReport data model. If we do not set the message property during a report operation, then the previously set message will be used.

The optional percentage property specifies the level of progress as a percentage and will be visualized with the progress bar. The value is an unsigned integer in the range [0, 100]. If the server does not set the initial value with the begin request, then the client will ignore the subsequent values set with the progress report notification.

In such cases, the user will be given the impression that the process will be running indefinitely. Therefore, it is for the best user experience that always tries to set the percentage property. The percentage property is also available with the WorkDoneProgressReport data model.

Report Progress

Once the server starts a progress with the begin notification, now the server has to update the progress. Progress updating will be done by the $/progress notification similar to the begin notification. The difference is the used payload. For the progress reporting notification, we use the WorkDoneProgressReport data model where the available properties are as follows.

The kind property specifies the progress notification kind. For the report notification, the value should be set to report.

The other available properties are cancellable, message, and percentage. We discussed these in the earlier section in detail, addressing the report notification as well.

End Progress

Now we have started the notification and reported the progress to the client. Once the operation is done, the server should notify the client that the particular long-running task is completed. This is achieved by sending the progress end notification to the client via the $/progress notification. The sent payload will distinguish between the begin, report, and end requests. The server sends the WorkDoneProgressEnd payload to the client for the progress end notification where the following fields are available.

The kind property specifies the progress notification kind. For the end notification, the value should be set to end.

The message property specifies the final message to be shown, stating the output of the operation. For example, in our use case, we can specify Successfully indexed 3 projects.

Implementing the Server-Initiated Progress

Now let's have a look at how we can create a server-initiated progress for an indexing implementation. As mentioned earlier, the client-initiated progress is associated with requests. The server-initiated progress is very useful for reporting progress for the tasks other than bound to the requests as in our example for indexing. In order to create and report the server-initiated progress, we follow the following sequence of operations:

1. Server sends the `workspace/workDoneProgress/create` notification.

    The server creates a UUID for the progress and sends with the notification.

2. Server sends the `$/progress` notification with **begin** parameters.

    The server uses the same UUID created in step 1.

3. Server sends the `$/progress` notification with **report** parameters.

    The server uses the same UUID created in step 1.

4. Server sends the `$/progress` notification with **end** parameters.

    The server uses the same UUID created in step 1.

One of the most important facts which we need to keep in mind is not to use the same UUID/token generated for a given progress with another progress report since the client uses the token to correlate progress notifications.

Listing 11-4 shows the example implementation for the indexing progress.

Listing 11-4. Implementing Server-Initiated WorkDoneProgress Support (BalWorkspaceService.java)

```
private void reIndexWorkspace(BalWorkspaceContext context,
                             LanguageClient client)
        throws ExecutionException, InterruptedException {
    List<Path> projectRoots = getAllProjectRoots(context);
    WorkDoneProgressCreateParams progressCreate =
            new WorkDoneProgressCreateParams();
    UUID uuid = UUID.randomUUID();
    progressCreate.setToken(uuid.toString());
    // Send the begin progress notification
    client.createProgress(progressCreate);

    // Notify the begin progress
    WorkDoneProgressBegin begin = new WorkDoneProgressBegin();
```

```
begin.setTitle("Indexing");
ProgressParams beginParams = new ProgressParams();
beginParams.setValue(Either.forLeft(begin));
beginParams.setToken(Either.forLeft(uuid.toString()));
client.notifyProgress(beginParams);

for (int i = 0; i < projectRoots.size(); i++) {
    WorkDoneProgressReport reportProgress =
            new WorkDoneProgressReport();
    reportProgress.setCancellable(false);
    reportProgress
            .setPercentage(((i + 1) / projectRoots.size()) * 100);
    reportProgress.setMessage((i + 1)
            + " out of " + projectRoots.size()
            + " projects being indexing");
    ProgressParams params = new ProgressParams();
    params.setToken(uuid.toString());
    params.setValue(Either.forLeft(reportProgress));
    client.notifyProgress(params);
    // Here goes the indexing logic.
    // For testing purposes we add a thread sleep
    try {
        Thread.sleep(2000);
    } catch (InterruptedException e) {
        // ignore
    }
}

// Notify Progress End
WorkDoneProgressEnd endProgress = new WorkDoneProgressEnd();
endProgress.setMessage("Successfully indexed "
        + projectRoots.size() + " projects");
ProgressParams endParams = new ProgressParams();
endParams.setToken(uuid.toString());
endParams.setValue(Either.forLeft(endProgress));
client.notifyProgress(endParams);
}
```

Partial Result Support

When it comes to considerably large projects, server implementations can take time to provide the completed result for a given operation. For example, consider the workspace/symbol where there are more than one project. In such cases, the servers tend to implement indexing and caching solutions on the server side for reducing the response time to the client, providing a better user experience. Sometimes, indexing and caching capabilities will not be ideal if caching is also going to take time as well as in scenarios where indexes and caches are supposed to be eventually consistent.

In order to solve this requirement, the Language Server Protocol introduces the partial result support. If we consider a given operation such as auto-completions, the server sends a list of `CompletionItems` as the response. With the partial result support, the protocol allows the servers to send the result of the `textDocument/completion` to be an n number of `CompletionItem` lists. If we clarify the behavior further, the partial result is sent via `$/progress` notifications, and we send n notifications where each notification carries a list of m `CompletionItems`. It is also important to note that once the server is done sending the response, it should send an empty response to specify that sending the result is done.

If the client supports partial results for a given operation, the client specifies with a token. In our example scenario, the CompletionParams includes the partialResultToken field. This token value should be used by the server in subsequent partial result notifications for the correlation.

Working with Launchers

At the beginning of this book, we learned that the Language Server Protocol is agnostic of the communication protocol. When implementing the Language Server, it is important to keep in mind that the server can be used by multiple clients, and these clients might use different programming languages and frameworks for the implementation. Furthermore, if we consider a cloud editor, the client cannot use conventional communication protocols to communicate with the server implementation. This is where the server implementation should be able to support more than one communication protocol and allow the client to choose the preferred communication method.

When we consider the most widely used communication protocols, we can specify the following. And also, Table 11-1 shows possible pros and cons of using these communication protocols:

1. Stdio – Using the standard input and output channels.

2. Pipe – Using Windows pipes/Unix socket files.

3. Socket – Using sockets opened on a given port.

4. node-ipc – Using the node interprocess communication (IPC). This can only be used when the server and the client are both implemented with a node.

Table 11-1. *Pros and Cons of Different Protocol usages*

Protocol	Pros	Cons
Standard I/O	Easy to set up and get started with	Some libraries can write logs to a standard I/O channel which can lead to breaking the communication stream
Pipe	Faster than server socket implementation	Flexibility when porting from one OS to another
Socket	Optimal for scenarios such as using WebSocket	The client should find a port to let the server know which port to start with
node-ipc	Higher performance and easy interoperability when both the server and the client are implemented with a node	Can only be used when using a node for both client and server implementations

This is where the concept of launchers comes. For convenience, the server can allow the client to specify the server's communication mode via command-line arguments. For example, the client can specify the port as a command-line argument.

In our example implementation, we have implemented two such launchers for the clients. Listing 11-5 shows the stdio launcher implementation.

Listing 11-5. Stdio Launcher Implementation

```
public class StdioLauncher {
    public static void main(String[] args) throws ExecutionException,
    InterruptedException {
        ...
        startServer(System.in, System.out);
    }

    public static void startServer(InputStream in, OutputStream out)
            throws InterruptedException, ExecutionException {
        BalLanguageServer server = new BalLanguageServer();
        Launcher<LanguageClient> launcher = LSPLauncher.
        createServerLauncher(server, in, out);
        server.connect(launcher.getRemoteProxy());
        Future<?> startListening = launcher.startListening();
        startListening.get();
    }
}
```

Now, let's have a look at the implementation in detail. The main method of the
StdioLauncher calls the startServer method with two arguments, the input stream
and the output stream, to read and write the protocol's messages. Here, we use the
standard system input stream and the standard system output stream as inputs. As
we mentioned in an earlier chapter, we use LSP4J[1] as the protocol implementation
library. As shown in Listing 11-5, first we create an instance of our Language Server
implementation (BallerinaLanguageServer) and use this instance to create a
server launcher instance as Launcher<LanguageClient> launcher = LSPLauncher.
createServerLauncher(server, in, out);. The LSP4J library is not only a Language
Server Protocol implementation, but its core is implemented in a more generic manner
which allows the developers to implement their own JSON-RPC servers and clients. As
an extension of that, the library provides us with LSPLauncher which creates a Language
Server implementation. Once we acquire the server launcher instance, we connect to

---

[1] https://github.com/eclipse/lsp4j

the server via the connect method. As an input, we need to provide the remote proxy instance for the acquired launcher. In the BalLanguageServer implementation, it is mandatory to override the connect method as in Listing 11-6.

Listing 11-6. BalLanguageServer Implements the connect Method

```
public class BalLanguageServer implements LanguageServer,
LanguageClientAware {
    ...
    private LanguageClient client;

    ...
    @Override
    public void connect(LanguageClient languageClient) {
        // Language client instance
        this.client = languageClient;
        this.serverContext.setClient(this.client);
    }
    ...
}
```

As you can see, we populate a variable called client within the connect method. If you can remember the examples we discussed in previous chapters, there are requests and notifications sent by the server to the client, such as workspace/workspaceFolders. In our implementation, we use APIs/methods which we can access through this particular client instance which is passed as the input. In other words, this is the remote proxy instance we accessed via the launcher we discussed in Listing 11-5. In the server implementation, it is important to cache this remote proxy/client instance when the connect method calls, since it is the most convenient way to get access to the client instance.

Note lsp4j is a Java implementation for the Language Server Protocol. This not only supports implementing Language Servers, but also the developers can use the provided generic APIs to implement other JSON-RPC servers. Also, the lsp4j library allows us to implement the clients.

Now let's have a look at a launcher implementation which allows the clients to connect via a socket. Listing 11-7 shows a Java socket-based launcher implementation.

Listing 11-7. Java Socket–Based Launcher Implementation

```java
public class TCPLauncher {

    public static void main(String[] args) {
        try {
            Socket clientSocket = new Socket("127.0.0.1", 9925);
            startServer(clientSocket.getInputStream(), clientSocket.
            getOutputStream());
        } catch (IOException | InterruptedException | ExecutionException e) {
            // Failed to start the server
        }
    }

    public static void startServer(InputStream in, OutputStream out)
            throws InterruptedException, ExecutionException {
        BalLanguageServer server = new BalLanguageServer();
        Launcher<LanguageClient> launcher = LSPLauncher.
        createServerLauncher(server, in, out);
        server.connect(launcher.getRemoteProxy());
        Future<?> startListening = launcher.startListening();
        startListening.get();
    }
}
```

As you can see, the startServer method implementation is the same as we discussed in the StdioLauncher implementation, in which the lsp4j is not aware of the communication protocol. The only difference in this approach is how we acquire the input and output streams for the communication. Within the main method, we create a Socket instance on the localhost and on port 9925. The input and output streams we use for the communication are the ones from the created socket. The socket input and output streams can be acquired from the socket's getInputStream and getOutputStream APIs, respectively.

For simplicity, we have hardcoded the port number within the code itself. But, this solution can be easily extended to be a generic solution where the port is going to be read from the command-line arguments.

Extension Points

Implementing and Extending Protocol Services

Up to this point, we have come a long way studying standard Language Server Protocol capabilities and their optimal usages when it comes to the implementation of a language smartness provider – a Language Server. If you look back, there are lots of features supported by the Language Server Protocol, and we can do so many things with those features. However, there can be certain scenarios where a programming language might need to implement a specific set of capabilities along with the Language Server Protocol implementation. How are we supposed to do that when it comes to a single client implementation?

Let's go back to the start of our journey where we discussed protocol basics. You can remember we discussed that the Language Server Protocol operates on top of JSON-RPC. In other words, we can consider the Language Server implementation as a JSON-RPC server implementation itself and the language client implementation as a JSON-RPC client implementation. Now, if we think further from this point, the Language Server Protocol can also be considered as a JSON-RPC server and client implementation with a defined set of request-response pairs and notifications. Also, this provides us the liberty to extend the protocol with new requests, responses, and notifications.

In our example implementation, we are going to implement a new request-response pair to get the syntax node information for a given position. Let's say the operation is `textDocument/parser/node`.

Request Parameters

Request parameters are the same as the request parameters we discussed in the `textDocument/completion` request, `TextDocumentPositionParams`. In the implementation, the server can get the document URI, line, and column to capture the position where the syntax node information is to be found.

Response Parameters

As a response, we define a new response data model as shown in Listing 11-8. The response NodeResponse has two fields.

The nodeKind specifies the syntax node kind for the found node at the given position. For example, if we consider a Ballerina function definition node, the syntax kind would be FUNCTION_DEFINITION.

The diagnostics property specifies a list of syntax diagnostic messages attached to the given node.

Listing 11-8. NodeResponse Data Model

```
public class NodeResponse {
    private String nodeKind;
    private List<String> diagnostics;

    public String getNodeKind() {
        return nodeKind;
    }

    public void setNodeKind(String nodeKind) {
        this.nodeKind = nodeKind;
    }

    public List<String> getDiagnostics() {
        return diagnostics;
    }

    public void setDiagnostics(List<String> diagnostics) {
        this.diagnostics = diagnostics;
    }
}
```

Implementing the Service

Now, if you look at the LanguageServer interface, you can see there are a bunch of APIs defined. Among those, we are going to focus on two special APIs, as in Listing 11-9.

Listing 11-9. LanguageServer Interface

```java
public interface LanguageServer {
    @JsonRequest
    CompletableFuture<InitializeResult> initialize(Initialize
    Params params);

    @JsonNotification
    default void initialized(InitializedParams params) {
        initialized();
    }

    @Deprecated
    default void initialized() {
    }

    @JsonRequest
    CompletableFuture<Object> shutdown();

    @JsonNotification
    void exit();

    @JsonDelegate
    TextDocumentService getTextDocumentService();

    @JsonDelegate
    WorkspaceService getWorkspaceService();

    @JsonNotification("window/workDoneProgress/cancel")
    default void cancelProgress(WorkDoneProgressCancelParams params) {
        throw new UnsupportedOperationException();
    }
}
```

As we discussed in earlier chapters, we could observe two main operation namespaces as textDocument and workspace where operations such as textDocument/ completion and workspace/symbol are defined. The getDocumentService and the getWorkspaceService are the two APIs which bind the service contracts with the client implementation during the startup.

Now, we are going to bind another namespace for our new service. In order to do so, we have to extend the `LanguageServer` interface and define a new API to access the new service. So, now our `ExtendedLanguageServer` interface will look like in Listing 11-10. You can refer to the actual implementation within the `extensions.service.parser` directory in the repository. Also, refer to Listing 11-11 for the new service interface for defining the namespace and the operation.

Listing 11-10. ExtendedLanguageServer Interface

```
public interface BalExtendedLanguageServer extends LanguageServer {
    @JsonDelegate
    BallerinaParserService getBallerinaParserService();
}
```

Listing 11-11. BallerinaParserService Interface Defining the Operation Namespace

```
@JsonSegment("textDocument/parser")
public interface BallerinaParserService {
    /**
     * Operation name would be picked as node and the client will
     * call the operation textDocument/parser/node
     *
     * @param params input parameters
     * @return node response
     */
    @JsonRequest
    CompletableFuture<NodeResponse> node(TextDocumentPositionParams params);
}
```

Supporting Multiple Languages

When we consider the Language Server Protocol, in general we consider a single document kind. For example, it could be JSON, TypeScript, or Ballerina. Even in the client implementation, we specify for which document type we are going to enable the particular extension.

When we consider modern programming languages, it is not only a single document type, but also there are different document types involved. For example, when we consider Ballerina, its platform includes toml configuration files for maintaining package information (`Ballerina.toml`), dependency information (`Dependencies.toml`), and so on. Even though the document type is different from each other, all of these share a single Ballerina platform. If you remember, we carried out various tasks such as refreshing code lenses upon the changes to the `Ballerina.toml` configuration file. Now consider that we need to provide auto-completion support for `Ballerina.toml` and `Dependencies.toml` configuration files. The first option that comes to mind is to have a Language Server implementation and create a separate extension. This is not scalable if there are more than one configuration file type. In order to solve this, what if we have a solution where we can provide auto-completion for more than one document type via a single Language Server implementation? Let's see how we can handle this requirement with a single Language Server implementation.

Dynamic Registration of Capabilities

As we discussed in earlier chapters, the Language Server Protocol allows us to dynamically register capabilities. One of the strengths in this capability is that the server can specify a document selector to register the given capability. If we refresh our memory, we discussed registering a file watcher for the Ballerina.toml configuration file to receive file watch events. Similarly, we can dynamically register the completion capability for `Ballerina.toml` configuration files with a document selector and also with all the server capabilities of `textDocument/completion`. Listing 11-12 shows you how to dynamically register the completion capability for `Ballerina.toml`.

Listing 11-12. Dynamically Register the Completion Capability for Ballerina.toml (DynamicCapabilitySetter.java)

```
public void registerBallerinaTomlCompletion(LSContext serverContext) {
    Optional<ClientCapabilities> clientCapabilities =
            serverContext.getClientCapabilities();

    if (clientCapabilities.isEmpty()) {
        // Client capabilities are not saved
        return;
    }
```

```
CompletionCapabilities completionCapabilities =
        clientCapabilities.get().getTextDocument().getCompletion();
if (!completionCapabilities.getDynamicRegistration()) {
    /*
    client does not support dynamic registration for
      completion. Gracefully fall back
     */
    return;
}
CompletionRegistrationOptions options =
        new CompletionRegistrationOptions();
DocumentFilter tomlFilter = new DocumentFilter();
tomlFilter.setLanguage("toml");
tomlFilter.setScheme("file");
tomlFilter.setPattern("/**/" + ProjectConstants.BALLERINA_TOML);

options.setResolveProvider(true);
options.setDocumentSelector(Collections.singletonList(tomlFilter));
String method = Method.COMPLETION.getName();

Registration reg = new Registration(method, method);
List<Registration> regList = Collections.singletonList(reg);
RegistrationParams regParams = new RegistrationParams(regList);

return regParams;
}
```

Implementing a Delegator Mechanism

Now, our previous option is a viable solution for our problem even though there is one drawback. In order to support this capability, the client should also support dynamic capability registration. If the client does not support dynamic capability registration, it is not possible to support the textDocument/completion feature for more than one document type. However, we can fulfill the same requirement with a simple fix. We are going to introduce a Java Service Provider Interface (Java SPI)–based delegator mechanism. In order to support this mechanism, the client only needs to register the extension for the required language identifiers.

In the delegator implementation, we are going to introduce an extension interface, `CompletionFeatureExtension`, which will be used by our singleton instance of the delegator, `LanguageFeatureExtensionDelegator`.

Each of the extension implementations is supposed to implement the `CompletionFeatureExtension` interface. Also, in order to support the SPI implementation, we are going to add the `META-INF/services/org.lsp.server.core.extensions.languages.LanguageFeatureExtensionDelegator` file and, for each of the implementation, an entry to the file as `org.lsp.server.core.extensions.languages.TomlCompletion`.

Now our extension delegator instance will look like in Listing 11-13.

Listing 11-13. LanguageExtensionDelegator Implementation

```
public class LanguageFeatureExtensionDelegator {
    private static final LanguageFeatureExtensionDelegator INSTANCE
            = new LanguageFeatureExtensionDelegator();
    private final List<CompletionFeatureExtension> completionExtensions =
            new ArrayList<>();

    /**
     * Get the completions.
     *
     * @param params completion parameters
     * @return {@link Either} completion results
     * @throws Throwable while executing the extension
     */
    public Either<List<CompletionItem>, CompletionList>
    completion(CompletionParams params, LSContext serverContext)
            throws Throwable {
        List<CompletionItem> completionItems = new ArrayList<>();
        for (CompletionFeatureExtension ext : completionExtensions) {
            if (ext.validate(params)) {
                completionItems.addAll(ext.completion(params,
                    serverContext));
            }
        }
    }
```

```
        return Either.forLeft(completionItems);
    }

    private LanguageFeatureExtensionDelegator() {
        this.loadCompletionExtensions();
    }

    private void loadCompletionExtensions() {
        ServiceLoader.load(CompletionFeatureExtension.class)
                .forEach(completionExtensions::add);
    }
}
```

As shown in the implementation, with this mechanism, the server can support more than one feature extension type, and the server implementation only has to add a corresponding API for the language feature as we have shown for the completion feature. As shown in Listing 11-13, the delegator implementation has an API (`completion()`) which is called within the service (`BalTextDocumentService`).

Note   Here, we are not going to talk about Java SPI implementation internals. The reader can refer to the official documentation[2] for implementation details.

Summary

In this chapter, we went through some of the advanced concepts we can introduce to a Language Server implementation. First, we looked at how the Language Server Protocol allows progress reporting. Progress reporting initiation can happen in two ways: server-initiated progress reporting and client-initiated progress reporting. Client-initiated progress reporting allows the server to report progress for language features which take time to complete. For example, the workspace/symbol operation can take a considerable time to complete, and the server can report the progress of the operation. On the other hand, server-initiated progress reporting allows the user to report progress for operations

---

[2] https://docs.oracle.com/javase/tutorial/sound/SPI-intro.html

outside of standard protocol features. In our example implementation, we looked at how we can report progress for a background indexing operation. The discussed concepts can be extended for features such as auto-downloading dependencies and cleanup tasks.

Then we had a look at the partial result support for language features such as references and completions. Similar to the work done progress support, partial results are also notified with progress notifications.

When it comes to the implementation and integration with clients, the server should be flexible, and clients should be able to communicate with the desired communication protocol, such as stdio, node-ipc, socket, or pipes.

Apart from that, we had a look at the ways we can extend the standard Language Server Protocol. We looked at registering new services for operation namespaces such as `textDocument` and `workspace`. Then we looked at how we can use the Language Server Protocol's built-in dynamic capability registration to support language features for more than one language such as for providing auto-completion support for both Ballerina and toml sources via the same server implementation. Also, we had a look at a delegator implementation to support the same requirement.

Index

A

Abstract syntax tree (AST), 158
Advanced concepts, server
      capabilities, 212

B

Base protocol
    content type, 18
    header value, 18
    language server, 18

C

Code fixes
    codeAction request
        client capabilities, 118
        command property, 124
        diagnostics, 123
        disabled property, 124
        execute command options, 118
        generation, 123
        isPreferred property, 124
        request parameters, 120
        resolve request, 125, 126
        response, 121
        server capabilities, 119
        VSCode's representation, 123
        workspace/executeCommand, 117
    codeLens request, 126
        client capabilities, 126
        range property, 127
        refresh request, 128
        resolve request, 128
        response generation, 127, 128
        server capabilities, 126
Command-line interface (CLI), 3

D

Debug Adapter Protocol (DAP), 25
Diagnostics
    auto-completion
        additionalTextEdits, 82
        client capabilities, 72–74
        completion items, 84
        content assist, 75–78
        documentation/additional
          information, 84–88
        features, 72
        function body completion, 76
        general request-response flow, 76
        insertion, 78–84
        server capabilities, 74, 75
        setTags method, 86
        sorting/filtering, 88, 89
    completionItem/resolve request, 89–92
    CompletionItemResolver utility, 91
    hover request, 97–100
    initialization/capabilities, 65–67
    ModulePartNodeContextProvider, 90
    publishing server, 68–73
    relatedInformation property, 66
    signatureHelp request, 92

233

Printed in the United States
by Baker & Taylor Publisher Services